One-Tier Party Cakes

First published in 2020

Search Press Limited
Wellwood, North Farm Road,
Tunbridge Wells, Kent TN2 3DR

ISBN: 978-1-78221-749-7

The Publishers and authors can accept no responsibility for
any consequences arising from the information, advice or
instructions given in this publication.

Readers are permitted to reproduce any of the items in this
book for their personal use, or for the purpose of selling for
charity, free of charge and without the prior permission of the
Publishers. Any use of the items for commercial purposes is
not permitted without the prior permission of the Publishers.

Suppliers
If you have difficulty in obtaining any of the materials and
equipment mentioned in this book, please visit the Search
Press website for details of suppliers: www.searchpress.com

You are invited to visit the author's website: lindyscakes.co.uk

Publishers' note
All the step-by-step photographs in this book feature the
author, Lindy Smith, demonstrating how to make and
decorate cakes. No models have been used.

A note from the author

As always, I love to see how I've inspired you so please
do add pictures of your creations to Pinterest, quoting
my name or this book so I can easily find them; Tweet on
Twitter using my Twitter handle @LindysCakes, or post
your photographs on the 'Lindy's Cakes' Facebook page.

ACKNOWLEDGEMENTS

Creating a book is always a time-consuming
process with many steps along the way,
from the initial in-depth researching and
experimenting to the eventual creating, writing,
photographing and editing. I would therefore
like to thank those who have helped me move
from one step to the next.

I would like to mention the generosity of
Renshaw for supplying me with sugarpaste,
modelling chocolate and Rainbow Dusts.
Without your wonderful products, covering
and decorating these cakes wouldn't have
been so easy. I would also like to thank Amy of
Sweet Stamp for supplying me with samples of
her beautiful letter embossers, which became
an integral part of my *Heart Design* cake;
also thank you to Stand It cake boards for the
gorgeous, subtly patterned board used on my
Klimt's Cat project.

Sarah Pickles, thank you for allowing me to
use your amazing story as inspiration for
the baby shower cake and thank you, Jane
Burkinshaw, for the photographs of Sarah.
A huge thank you goes to my friends Jill Ming
and Elaine Henshaw for providing me with
the dancing-in-the-rain inspiration and taking
me to Skomer to see the puffins. Thank you
to Jill and Heather Nobel for allowing me to
use photographs of your adorable cats for
the *Klimt's Cat* inspirations board. I'd also like
to thank my Facebook supporters for their
continued support and valuable suggestions
through the whole process of putting this
book together.

Finally, I'd like to thank the team at Search Press
for allowing me a huge amount of creative
freedom and for letting me develop and
implement my ideas.

Lindy Smith is an established author of 15 cake decorating books including the best-selling *The Contemporary Cake Decorating Bible*, and *Creative Colour for Cake Decorating*, which won an International Gourmand Cookbook Award. Lindy loves to teach and travels to many parts of the globe sharing her skills and knowledge through hands-on classes and demonstrations both large and small. She has appeared on television many times. Lindy lives in rural Shropshire, UK, an area that has inspired many of the cakes in this book. Visit her website www.lindyscakes.co.uk

One-Tier Party Cakes

12 stunning cakes for special occasions

SEARCH PRESS

CONTENTS

Welcome Home 28

Heart Design 38

Dancing in the Rain 46

Dandelion Clock 54

Brenda the
Brandhill Sheep 64

'Sarah's Miracle':
Baby Shower 76

INTRODUCTION

Designing and creating cakes is my passion. I absolutely love how sugarcraft allows me to experiment with my creativity, dreaming up and bringing new cake designs to life. One of my favourite sayings is, 'Creativity is intelligence having fun' – I've certainly had fun creating these designs for you.

For me, physically decorating the cakes is often the easiest part of working on a book: the biggest challenge, and often the most thrilling part, is the creative process – the thinking, questioning and playing with design ideas. Sometimes this can take quite a while, although very occasionally a fully formed idea can just appear, such as my *Toadstools* cake (see pages 122–129). When an idea has taken shape, it's time to start experimenting and testing to see what works and what does not. Often a particular design can be executed in a number of different ways. I think it's important to try to find the best approach and the most suitable techniques. Usually, I work out my ideas on experimental boards before finalizing which way to go. I hope that the finished designs appeal to you, and that you have fun with them.

After all the years that I've been creating cakes and teaching, I know that baking and decorating a cake can be very therapeutic. As with all arts and crafts, it can take you away from the everyday – provided, of course, that you allow yourself enough time. Being focused on something creative and beautiful is very absorbing and calming. The cake projects in this book have been designed to challenge you but also to be achievable. They are projects to immerse yourself in, ones where you can enjoy the process as well as the results. The theme for these designs is celebrations and parties – now, who doesn't have something to celebrate? I believe we all do!

As you will notice, all the designs are double- or even triple-height cakes, and all have sharp top edges. I have featured methods to create these effects in the Techniques section, so please do refer to these if you need to. I've tried to include as many new decorating techniques as I can, from cocoa butter painting or working with modelling chocolate to airbrushing techniques and using a fluid writer. My hope is that I've included something new that you'd like to try.

To see more of my designs and to look for cake inspiration, please visit my website, lindyscakes.co.uk, where there is a wealth of examples just waiting for you to discover. Click on the galleries and the blog to see cakes in all shapes, sizes and colours. Happy sugarcrafting!

Sweet wishes,

Lindy

EQUIPMENT AND TOOLS

You will find the following equipment useful when baking and decorating
your cakes. Any specialist sugarcraft equipment – such as embossers, cutters
and moulds – can be seen in the projects throughout the book.

BAKING EQUIPMENT AND TOOLS

- **Electric mixer with K beater** Use to mix up cake batters;
- **Bowls in various sizes** Use to mix together cake ingredients;
- **Baking parchment** This can be used to line **cake tins**;
- **Palette knife** Use this for spreading buttercream and ganache;
- **Wooden spoon** Use to mix buttercream, ganache and so on;
- **Measuring spoons** These are useful for accurate measurement of ingredients;

- **Spatula** This tool can be used for scraping out bowls;
- **Pair of scissors** Cut your baking parchment to size;
- **Chef's bowls** Use these for measuring out ingredients;
- **Wire rack** Place your cakes on these racks to cool.

DECORATING EQUIPMENT AND TOOLS

- **Cake boards;**
- **Carving knives** These sharp, long-bladed pastry knives are used for levelling and torting cakes (see page 19);
- **Palette knives** Use these for cutting paste and adding texture;
- **Cocktail sticks/toothpicks** Use these to add small amounts of paste colour to icing;
- **Paintbrushes** A range of sizes is useful for painting and dusting, from a large, flat brush to a fine-tipped brush;
- **Piping tubes** These are for use in a sugar shaper, or to cut out small circles;
- **Rolling pins, both large and small** These are ideal for rolling out different types of paste;
- **Scissors** Trim your paste to shape;
- **Metal ruler (not shown)** Use with a craft knife to cut straight edges;
- **5mm spacers** Use when rolling out sugarpaste (fondant);
- **1mm spacers** Use these smaller spacers for rolling out modelling paste;
- **Self-healing cutting mat** Use this in conjunction with a craft knife when cutting out intricate templates;

- **Spirit level;**
- **Pro-froster (rear left)** Ensure that your crumb-coated cake has vertical sides and a horizontal top;
- **Ball tool** Use this to soften the edges of petals;
- **Craft knife** This is ideal for intricate cutting tasks;
- **Cutting wheel** This can be used instead of a knife to avoid dragging the paste;
- **Dresden tool** Create decorative markings on paste;
- **Scriber** Use this tool to scribe around templates, pop air bubbles in paste and remove small sections of paste;
- **Smoother** Create a smooth and even finish to sugarpaste (fondant);
- **Sugar shaper and discs** Create pieces of uniformly shaped modelling paste by extruding the paste through discs with different-size holes;
- **Silicone modelling tools** For working with modelling chocolate;
- **Non-stick work board** Use this surface for rolling out pastes;
- **Airbrushing tool** Add background colours to sugarpaste (fondant);
- **Set square** Use this to ensure your designs are straight.

RECIPES

The cake under the icing is vitally important – it needs to be moist, able to support the added weight of the icing and, above all, taste fantastic.

On the following pages is a collection of my tried-and-tested recipes for you to experiment with. Each recipe should bake you a cake that is 7.5cm (3in) deep, so for each design, you'll need to bake two or three cakes of the same size and stack them following the instructions on page 19. I've included quantities for larger cakes as well, so you can see what ingredients you need. Although you will be keen to get started on one of these fantastic cake projects, take a little time to read this section to familiarize yourself with some of the basics. This will help you achieve good results. If your cake is to be a creation to be proud of, you will need to be fully prepared. Before you start any of the projects, read through the instructions carefully so you understand what is involved and how much time to allow. Make sure you have all the materials and equipment to hand before you begin.

TIME PLANNING

Try not to leave everything to the last moment – these are not quick cakes, so enjoy the process, and ensure that you allow sufficient time in which to create them.

Cakes baked from the recipes in this book last for about two weeks. I advise that you allow one week to decorate and another to eat, but if you need more time to decorate, that is not a problem as long as you plan in advance.

LINING TINS

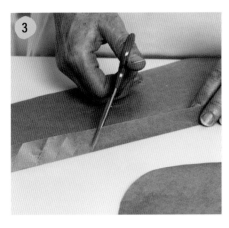

There are cake release sprays on the market which you can use but I still prefer this traditional method of lining tins. Neatly lined tins will prevent the cake mixture from sticking and help ensure a good shape. Use a good-quality baking parchment paper that is designed for the purpose. The paper should always sit right up against the sides of the tin with no large air pockets. Also, ensure that the uppermost side edge does not fold down into the cake – secure it in place with a little fat or a small fold in the paper.

1. Place your tin on the top of the baking parchment. Draw around the base with a pencil and cut out the resulting circle with scissors.

2. Measure the circumference of your tin and cut a strip of baking parchment slightly longer than this measurement to allow for an overlap. Make the strip 5cm (2in) deeper than the height of the tin. Fold up 2.5cm (1in) along the bottom of the strip.

3. Make diagonal cuts into the folded-over section of the paper that goes around the sides to enable the paper to sit snugly around the sides of the tin.

4. Grease the tin. Place the strip around the sides with the cut edge at the bottom, then place the parchment circle for the base on top.

CAKE RECIPES

MADEIRA CAKE

A firm, moist cake that can be flavoured to suit – see 'Flavourings', below. This cake is ideal for both carving and covering with sugarpaste (fondant) and will keep for up to two weeks.

METHOD

1. Preheat the oven to 160°C/Fan 140–150°C/325°F/Gas mark 2–3.

2. Grease and line the cake tins with baking parchment. To prevent the sides crusting and the top doming, you can tie a double layer of brown paper or newspaper around the outside of the tin.

3. Cream the butter and sugar in a large mixing bowl until light, fluffy and very pale. I find that this takes about five minutes in a mixer. Sift the flours together in a separate bowl.

4. The eggs should be at room temperature. Break each egg carefully into a separate cup to prevent small pieces of eggshell falling into the batter. Beat the eggs into the creamed mixture, one at a time, following each with a spoonful of flour to prevent the mixture curdling.

5. Sift the remaining flour into the creamed mixture and fold in carefully with a large metal spoon. Add the flavouring, if you are using any. At this stage, you can add glycerine. You will need ¼tsp per egg, as it helps to keep the cake moist.

6. Transfer to the lined tin and bake for the time given in the table below. When the cakes are ready, they will be well risen, firm to the touch, and a skewer inserted into the centre will come out clean.

7. Leave the cakes to cool in the tins; then, leaving any lining paper on, wrap the cake in foil or place in an airtight container for at least twelve hours before levelling, to allow the cake to settle.

Flavourings

Traditionally, Madeira cake was flavoured with lemon, but it can also be made with other flavourings. Flavourings are given for a six-egg-quantity Madeira cake; increase or decrease the amounts for other quantities.

- Lemon: grated rind of two lemons;
- Vanilla: 5ml (1tsp) vanilla extract;
- Cherry: 350g (12oz) glacé (candied) cherries, halved;
- Fruit: 350g (12oz) sultanas (golden raisins), currants, raisins or dates;
- Coconut: 110g (4oz) desiccated (dry, unsweetened, shredded) coconut;
- Almond: 5ml (1tsp) almond essence (extract) and 45ml (3tbsp) ground almonds.

Cake sizes			Unsalted (sweet) butter	Caster (super-fine) sugar	Self-raising flour	Plain (all-purpose) flour	Eggs, large (US extra large)	Baking times for one cake 7.5cm (3in) high at 160°C/ Fan 140–150°C/325°F/ Gas mark 2–3
7.5cm (3in) high cake	15cm (6in) high cake	22.5cm (9in) high cake						
12.5cm (5in) round			115g (4oz)	115g (4oz)	115g (4oz)	50g (1¾oz)	2	¾–1 hour
15cm (6in) round			175g (6oz)	175g (6oz)	175g (6oz)	75g (3oz)	3	1–1¼ hours
18cm (7in) round	2 × 12.5cm (5in) round		225g (8oz)	225g (8oz)	225g (8oz)	125g (4oz)	4	1–1¼ hours
20cm (8in) round	2 × 15cm (6in) round	3 × 12.5cm (5in) round	350g (12oz)	350g (12oz)	350g (12oz)	175g (6oz)	6	1¼–1½ hours
23cm (9in) round	2 × 18cm (7in) round		450g (1lb)	450g (1lb)	450g (1lb)	225g (8oz)	8	1½–1¾ hours
25.5cm (10in) round		3 × 15cm (6in) round	500g (1lb 2oz)	500g (1lb 2oz)	500g (1lb 2oz)	250g (9oz)	9	1½–1¾ hours

DELICIOUS CHOCOLATE FUDGE CAKE

As the name suggests, this is a delicious, moist, chocolate cake, ideal for covering with sugarpaste (fondant). The secret with this recipe is to use good-quality chocolate with a high cocoa solid content, if possible. Don't be tempted to use cheap, low-cocoa-solid chocolate or supermarket baking chocolate; you simply will not achieve the rich depth of flavour that this cake demands! This cake will keep up for about ten days.

Remember, all ovens are different, so do check your cake towards the end of its baking time.

METHOD

1. Preheat the oven to 160°C/Fan 140–150°C/315°F/Gas mark 2–3.

2. Slowly melt the butter, chocolate, coffee, sugar and water in a pan; once melted, allow to cool.

3. Add the eggs, oil and sour cream to the chocolate mix and stir well.

4. Sift all the dry ingredients into a large mixing bowl and make a well in the centre.

5. Pour the chocolate mixture into the well and mix until thoroughly combined.

6. Pour the batter into the lined tin and bake for the required time or until a skewer inserted into the centre of the cake comes out clean.

7. Leave the cake to cool in the tin.

Round cake sizes						
7.5cm- (3in-) high cake	12.5cm (5in)	15cm (6in)	18cm (7in)	20cm (8in)	23cm (9in)	25.5cm (10in)
15cm- (6in-) high cake			2 × 12.5cm (5in)	2 × 15cm (6in)	2 × 18cm (7in)	
22.5cm- (9in-) high cake				3 × 12.5cm (5in)		3 × 15cm (6in)
Unsalted butter	110g (4oz)	140g (5oz)	180g (6⅜oz)	225g (8oz)	280g (9⅞oz)	340g (12oz)
Good-quality chocolate	110g (4oz)	140g (5oz)	180g (6⅜oz)	225g (8oz)	280g (9⅞oz)	340g (12oz)
Instant coffee granules	1½tsp	2tsp	2¼tsp	1tbsp (15ml)	1¼tbsp	1½tbsp
Caster sugar or soft brown sugar	225g (8oz)	280g (10oz)	360g (12¾oz)	450g (1lb)	560g (1¼lb)	675g (1½lboz)
Water	75ml (2⅝fl. oz)	95ml (3⅜fl.oz)	120ml (4¼oz)	150ml (5¼fl.oz)	190ml (6¾fl.oz)	225ml (8oz)
4 large eggs	2	2.5	3	4	5	6
Vegetable oil	20ml (¾fl.oz)	20ml (¾fl.oz)	30ml (1fl.oz)	35ml (1¼fl.oz)	45ml (1⅝fl.oz)	50ml (1¾fl.oz)
Sour cream (or natural yoghurt or crème fraiche)	50ml (1¾fl.oz)	60ml (2⅛fl.oz)	80ml (2⅞fl.oz)	100ml (3½fl.oz)	125ml (4⅜fl.oz)	150ml (5¼fl.oz)
Self raising flour	60g (2⅛oz)	80g (2⅞oz)	100g (3½oz)	125g (4⅜oz)	160g (5⅝oz)	190g (6¾oz)
Plain flour	60g (2⅛oz)	80g (2⅞oz)	100g (3½oz)	125g (4⅜oz)	160g (5⅝oz)	190g (6¾oz)
Cocoa powder	25g (⅞oz)	30g (1oz)	40g (1⅜oz)	50g (1¾oz)	65g (2¼oz)	75g (2⅝oz)
Bicarbonate of soda	¼tsp	¼tsp	⅜tsp	½tsp	½tsp	¾tsp
Baking time for one 7.5cm- (3in-) deep cake	1 hour 10 minutes	1 hour 15 minutes	1 hour 30 minutes	1 hour 45 minutes	2 hours	2 hours 10mins

SUGAR AND CHOCOLATE RECIPES

Most of the sugar and chocolate recipes used in the book for covering, modelling and decoration can be made easily at home.

Sugarpaste (fondant): pinks unkneaded, white and green kneaded and beautifully smooth.

SUGARPASTE (FONDANT)

Sugarpaste (rolled fondant or roll-out icing) is used to cover cakes; ready-made sugarpaste can be obtained from supermarkets and cake-decorating suppliers, and is available in white – and the whole colour spectrum. It is also easy and inexpensive to make your own.

INGREDIENTS

Makes 1kg (2¼lb)

- 60ml (4tbsp) cold water
- 20ml (4tsp or 1 sachet) powdered gelatine
- 125ml (4⅜fl.oz) liquid glucose
- 15ml (1tbsp) glycerine
- 1kg (2¼lb) icing (confectioners') sugar, sieved, plus extra for dusting

METHOD

1. Place the water in a small bowl, sprinkle in the gelatine and soak until spongy. Stand the bowl over a pan of hot but not boiling water and stir until the gelatine is dissolved. Add the glucose and glycerine, stirring until well blended and runny.

2. Put the icing sugar in a large bowl. Make a well in the centre and slowly pour in the liquid ingredients, stirring constantly. Mix well. Turn out onto a surface dusted with icing sugar and knead until smooth, sprinkling with extra icing sugar if the paste becomes too sticky. The paste can be used immediately or tightly wrapped and stored in a food-grade plastic bag until required.

MODELLING PASTE

Modelling paste is used to add the decorations to many of the cakes in this book. This versatile paste keeps its shape well and dries harder than pure sugarpaste (fondant). Although there are many commercial pastes available, I still make my own as it is easy, cheap and very quick to do so.

If your sugarpaste (fondant) already contains gum (as many professional pastes now do), you'll need to add less gum (below). I usually buy cheaper sugarpastes (fondants) with no added gum to make my modelling pastes.

You will begin to feel a difference in the paste after an hour or so, but it is best left overnight. The modelling paste should be firm but pliable with a slightly elastic texture. Kneading the modelling paste makes it warm and easy to work with.

INGREDIENTS

Makes 225g (8oz)

- 225g (8oz) sugarpaste (fondant) in colours of your choice
- 5ml (1tsp) gum tragacanth

METHOD

1. Make a well in the sugarpaste and add the gum tragacanth.

2. Knead in the gum tragacanth.

3. Wrap in a plastic bag and allow the gum to work before use.

See page 26 for instructions on colouring sugarpaste (fondant) and modelling paste.

Modelling paste tips

- Always colour your sugarpaste (fondant) before adding the gum tragacanth.

- If time is short use CMC/Tylose instead of gum tragacanth: this is the synthetic version of gum tragacanth and works almost straight away. The downside of using CMC is that is doesn't set quite as firmly.

- Place your modelling paste in a microwave for a few seconds – this is an excellent way of warming it for use.

- If your paste is crumbly or too hard to work, add a touch of white vegetable fat (shortening) and a little boiled water, and knead until softened.

- If you have previously added a large amount of colour to your paste and it is consequently very soft, add an extra pinch or two of gum tragacanth.

MODELLING CHOCOLATE

The *'Sarah's Miracle': Baby Shower* (see pages 76–85) and *Puffy the Puffin* (see pages 102–111) cakes both use modelling chocolate. It is a relatively new product in modern cake decorating terms. The big advantages that it has over its sugar equivalent are that any joins can be easily blended away with the heat of a finger, it sticks to itself, sets firmly, is fairly robust and doesn't get affected by moisture. However, it isn't suitable if you live in a hot climate or have particularly hot hands – as it is chocolate, it melts readily. I'm lucky to have cold hands so this medium works a treat for me.

For the two projects in this book that feature modelling chocolate, I've used Renshaw's – however, it is not difficult to make your own. You may find that when you come to use your modelling chocolate it is rock solid. Simply heat it in a microwave for five-second bursts until it is warm enough to work. If the modelling chocolate gets too soft when you are handling it, stop. Allow the modelling chocolate to rest and cool down before resuming.

INGREDIENTS

For 'Sarah's Miracle: Baby Shower', pages 76–85

- 250g (9oz) white chocolate
- 65ml (2¼fl.oz) golden syrup or light corn syrup

For 'Puffy the Puffin', pages 102–111

- 150g (5¼oz) white chocolate
- 40ml (1½fl.oz) golden syrup or light corn syrup

METHOD

1. Melt your chocolate in a microwave in thirty-second bursts until completely melted.

2. Heat your golden syrup or light corn syrup for about thirty seconds in the microwave.

3. Pour your syrup into your melted chocolate and stir just enough to mix the chocolate through. Don't over-mix or the fat will separate.

4. Tip out onto plastic food wrap and wrap up well.

5. Leave at room temperature overnight to firm up or, if you are in a hurry, put it in the fridge for a couple of hours.

See page 27 for instructions on colouring modelling chocolate.

The ingredients and tools required to make modelling chocolate, plus two types of ready-made modelling chocolate in the foreground – milk and white.

FLOWER PASTE (PETAL/GUM PASTE)

This is used to make the delicate echinacea flowers on pages 112–121. Flower paste is available from commercial sugarcraft suppliers and can be bought in white and a variety of colours. There are many brands available, so try a few to see which you prefer. Alternatively, it is possible to make your own, but it is a time-consuming process and you will need a heavy-duty mixer.

Using flower pas

Flower paste dries quickly, so
remainder. Work it well with
If it is too hard and crumbly,
drying process and the egg

Best to buy these pastes as they are very heavy on mixing machines!

INGREDIENTS

Makes 600g (1lb 5oz)

- 500g (1lb 2oz) icing (confectioners') sugar
- 15ml (1tbsp) gum tragacanth
- 25ml (1½tbsp) cold water
- 10ml (2tsp) powdered gelatine
- 10ml (2tsp) liquid glucose
- 15ml (1tbsp) white vegetable fat (shortening) – see page 17
- 1 medium egg white

METHOD

1. Sieve the icing sugar and gum tragacanth into the greased mixing bowl of a heavy-duty mixer (the grease eases the strain on the machine).

2. Place the water in a small bowl, sprinkle in the gelatine and soak until spongy. Stand the bowl over a pan of hot but not boiling water and stir until the gelatine is dissolved. Add the glucose and white fat to the gelatine and continue heating until all the ingredients are melted and mixed.

3. Add the glucose mixture and egg white to the icing sugar. Beat the mixture very slowly until mixed – at this stage it will be a beige colour – then increase the speed to maximum until the paste becomes white and stringy.

4. Grease your hands and remove the paste from the bowl. Pull and stretch the paste several times, then knead together. Place in a food-grade plastic bag and store in an airtight container. Leave the paste to mature for at least twelve hours.

PASTILLAGE

The deer for the *Winter Wonderland* cake are made from pastillage. Pastillage is a very useful paste because, unlike modelling paste, it sets extremely hard and is not affected by moisture the way many other pastes are. However, the paste crusts quickly and is brittle once dry. You can buy it in powdered form, to which you add water, but it is easy to make yourself.

INGREDIENTS

Makes 350g (12oz)

- 1 egg white
- 300g (11oz) icing (confectioners') sugar, sifted
- 10ml (2tsp) gum tragacanth

METHOD

1. Put the egg white into a large mixing bowl. Gradually add enough icing sugar until the mixture combines together into a ball. Mix in the gum tragacanth, and then turn the paste out onto a work board or work surface and knead the pastillage well.

2. Incorporate the remaining icing sugar into the remainder of pastillage to give a stiff paste. Store pastillage in a food-grade plastic bag placed in an airtight container in a fridge for up to one month.

BUTTERCREAM

Buttercream has many uses: in this book, I use it as a crumb coat (see page 21), a filling between layers of cake, and also as a glue for sugarpaste (fondant).

These standard and white chocolate buttercream recipes are very easy to make.

INGREDIENTS: STANDARD BUTTERCREAM

- 110g (4oz) unsalted (sweet) butter
- 350g (12oz) icing (confectioners') sugar
- 15–30ml (1–2tbsp) milk or water
- A few drops of vanilla extract or alternative flavouring (see below, left)

METHOD

Place the butter in a bowl and beat until light and fluffy. Sift the icing sugar into the bowl and continue to beat until the mixture changes colour. Add just enough milk or water to give a firm but spreadable consistency. Flavour by adding the vanilla or an alternative, then store the buttercream in an airtight container until required.

Flavouring buttercream

Try replacing the liquid in the recipes with:
- Alcohols such as whisky, rum or brandy;
- Other liquids such as coffee, lemon curd, fresh fruit purees.

Alternatively, you can add:
- Nut butters to make a praline flavour;
- Flavours such as mint or rose extract.

INGREDIENTS: WHITE CHOCOLATE BUTTERCREAM

This is my family's favourite filling: it is wonderful used with my rich chocolate fudge cake recipe (see page 12).

- 115g (4oz) white chocolate
- 115g (4oz) unsalted (sweet) butter
- 225g (8oz) icing sugar

METHOD

Melt the chocolate in a bowl over hot water or in a microwave, in thirty-second bursts, and leave to cool slightly. Soften the butter and beat in the sugar, and then beat in the chocolate.

CHOCOLATE GANACHE

Used as a filling or coating, ganache is ideal for cakes as it sets firm, which makes covering cakes with sugarpaste (fondant) easier. Ganache is a must for all chocoholics – use the best-quality chocolate that you can source.

INGREDIENTS: DARK CHOCOLATE GANACHE

- 400g (14oz) dark chocolate
- 400ml (14fl.oz) cream

WHITE CHOCOLATE GANACHE

- 400g (14oz) white chocolate
- 160ml (5⅜fl.oz) cream

METHOD

Melt the chocolate and cream together in a bowl over a saucepan of gently simmering water, stirring to combine. Alternatively, use a microwave on low power, stirring every twenty seconds or so.

The ganache can be used warm once it has thickened slightly and is of a pouring consistency, or it can be left to cool so that it can be spread with a palette knife. Alternatively, once cooled completely, it can be whisked to give a lighter texture.

ROYAL ICING

Royal icing is available commercially; however, you can use this recipe for quick and easy tasks when only a little royal icing is required or when you need a strong glue.

INGREDIENTS

- 1 large egg white
- 250g (9oz) icing (confectioners') sugar, sifted

> **Note**
>
> You can replace fresh egg whites with dried albumen if you prefer.

METHOD

1. Put the egg white in a bowl, lightly beat it to break it down, then gradually beat in the icing sugar until the icing is glossy and forms soft peaks.

2. Store your royal icing in an airtight container; cover the top surface with plastic food wrap and a clean, damp cloth to prevent the icing forming a crust before sealing the lid and placing the container in a fridge.

3. Before use, bring to room temperature and paddle the icing on your work board with a palette knife to remove any trapped air bubbles.

PROFESSIONAL ROYAL ICING

For intricate piping details, it's well worth going to the effort of making professional icing. Use this recipe for *Puffy the Puffin* (see pages 102–111).

Make sure that all your equipment is spotless: even small residues of grease will affect your icing. Separate the egg whites the day before they are needed, sieve through a fine sieve or tea strainer, cover and then place in a fridge to allow the egg whites to strengthen.

INGREDIENTS

- 90g (3oz) free-range egg white (approximately 3 eggs)
- 455g (1lb) icing (confectioners') sugar, sifted
- 5–7 drops of lemon juice, if using fresh eggs

METHOD

1. Pla... ...the food of a mixer, s... in the icing sugar and add t... lemon juice.

2. Us... ...with heat as slowly as possible for between ten and twen... ...akes will d... ...take care to the consistency of the... ...icing forms a peak that bend... slightly it is at the... ...consistency.

[handwritten note overlaid: TREX. – has no smell & lovely + white]

3. St... your royal icing in an airtight container; cover the top surface with plast... ...and then a clean damp cloth to prevent the icing forming a crust, befo... sealing the lid and placing in a fridge. Bring to room temperature before using again.

ADDITIONAL EDIBLES

GLUES

You can often simply use water to stick your sugar decorations to your cakes. However, if you find you need something a little stronger, here are two options:

SUGAR GLUE

This is a quick, easy instant glue to make and is my preferred choice.

Break up pieces of white modelling paste into a small container and cover with boiling water. Stir until dissolved. This produces a thick, strong glue, which can be easily thinned by adding some more cooled boiled water. If a stronger glue is required, use pastillage rather than modelling paste as the base: this is useful for delicate work.

GUM GLUE

Clear gum glue is available commercially, often known as edible glue, but it is very easy and cheap to make yourself. The basic ingredients are: one part CMC to twenty parts warm water, which translates into ¼tsp to 2tbsp warm water.

Place the CMC into a small container with a lid, add the warm water, close the lid and shake well. Leave in the fridge overnight. In the morning, you will have a thick, clear glue that can be used to stick your sugar work together.

FATS

WHITE VEGETABLE FAT

This is a solid white vegetable fat (shortening) that is often known by a brand name: in the UK, Trex; in South Africa, Holsum; in Australia, Copha; and in the USA, Crisco. These products are more or less interchangeable in cake making.

COCOA BUTTER

Cocoa butter is a pure, stable fat that is pressed out of cacao beans. It has the flavour and aroma of cocoa. For decorating cakes, it is melted, mixed with coloured food dusts and then used as a paint. I find cocoa butter a very effective, easy way of painting detailed patterns and images onto cakes. I think of cocoa butter as the oil paint of the cake decorating world.

TECHNIQUES

COVERING CAKES

Follow these basic techniques to achieve a neat and professional appearance with your initial cake coverings. With care and practice, you will soon find that you have a perfectly smooth finish.

LEVELLING THE CAKES

Making an accurate cake base is an important part of creating your masterpiece. Here are two ways in which to do this:

1. USING A BAKING TIN

Place a cake board into the base of the tin in which the cake was baked so that when the cake is placed back on top, the outer edge of the cake will be level with the tin and the dome will protrude above.

With a long, sharp knife, cut the dome from the cake, keeping the knife against the tin. This will ensure that the cake is completely level.

2. USING A SET SQUARE

Place a set square up against the edge of the cake and, with cocktail sticks, mark the top of the cake at the required height. The recipes in the book should give you a cake that can be levelled at a height of 7–7.5cm (2¾–3in). With a large serrated knife, cut at the marked line and across the cake to remove the domed crust.

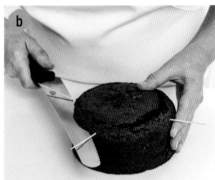

FILLING AND STACKING THE CAKES

It is not always necessary to add fillings to your cakes; however, many people like to fill their cakes with complementary flavours such as chocolate and orange ganache, praline buttercream or delicious homemade lemon curd.

To add fillings, split your cakes into a number of horizontal layers and spread with your choice of filling, setting it in the fridge if required. This splitting and filling process is known as 'torting'.

When choosing fillings, bear in mind that your cakes have to support the weight of the sugarpaste (fondant) and the decoration, so thin layers or layers that set firm are preferable.

To create the double- or triple-height cakes required for the designs in this book you will need to stack one or two cakes on top of one another. Do this by adding a suitable filling between the two cakes and set if appropriate. Use a set square to ensure that the sides are straight, adjusting the shape with a carving knife if not. Ensure that the cake is level by placing a cake board on top of the cake before testing with a spirit level.

Note that if you are planning to use chocolate ganache under your sugarpaste (fondant), you don't need to be quite as precise at this stage.

Tip

Before separating the two halves of your cake, make a vertical knife cut into the side of the cake so that you can easily replace the top half in the same position.

METHOD

1. Cut each of your cakes in half horizontally and spread your choice of filling evenly over one half. Carefully place the second half back into its original position, ensuring that the top of the cake is still level.

2. Once you have filled your cakes, spread a layer of filling over the top of one before stacking the next cake on top.

3. Adjust the positions of the cakes, ensuring that the sides are vertical and the top level – you may find a set square and spirit level useful.

4. Once you are happy with how the stacked cake looks, use a palette knife to smooth any excess filling around the sides of the cake. Finally, place the cake in a fridge to set – ideally, the filling needs to set firm.

COVERING A CAKE WITH CHOCOLATE GANACHE

Chocolate ganache is a delicious alternative to buttercream, especially when using chocolate cake. The great advantage of using ganache is that it sets firmly so adds stability to your cakes. The disadvantage is that it takes a little longer to apply as the two layers of ganache have to set.

Make your ganache (see page 16) and allow it to set. Once set, mix and soften the ganache until it is smooth and spreads easily. Attach your cake to its board, using a little ganache. Place the cake in a freezer for a few minutes to set before covering.

(see page 16)

Tip

Use a white chocolate ganache for cakes that are to be covered with a light-coloured sugarpaste (fondant).

METHOD

1. Using a palette knife, roughly cover the sides and top with a thick layer of ganache, making sure that there are no air pockets.

2. Take off the excess with the palette knife. Redistribute the excess ganache from the top edge onto the top of the cake. Place the cake in a freezer for a few minutes to allow the layer of ganache to set.

3. Add a second layer of ganache. Use a side-scraper to ensure that the finish is perfectly smooth, the cake sides vertical and the top level. Set in a freezer.

4. To attach sugarpaste to a ganached cake, simply brush hot water, sugar syrup (which can be flavoured) or piping gel over the cake to act as glue.

Tip

If your ganache is too hard, place in a microwave for a few seconds at a time to help soften it.

COVERING A CAKE WITH BUTTERCREAM

A buttercream covering or crumb coating is the traditional way to prepare a sponge cake that is to be covered with sugarpaste (fondant). The buttercream layer helps create an even surface and seals in the crumbs.

See page 16 for my buttercream recipes.

Tip

Apply just before covering a cake with sugarpaste (fondant) so that the buttercream acts as a glue.

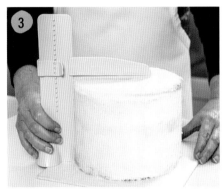

METHOD

1. Beat your buttercream until it is of a soft and spreadable consistency.

2. Using a palette knife, cover the cake with a thin layer of buttercream. Use the buttercream to fill in any holes and create a smooth surface on which to place the sugarpaste layer.

3. Use a pro-froster or similar tool to ensure you have created vertical sides and a horizontal top.

4. Warm a palette knife in hot water and use it to smooth the surface of your icing.

COVERING A CAKE WITH SUGARPASTE (FONDANT)

Once your cake is covered with buttercream or ganache it is ready to be covered in sugarpaste (fondant). The current trend is to make tall cakes with sharp edges. Many sugarpaste manufacturers have responded to this and have created pastes with added gum that allow us to cover tall cakes in one go and achieve these sought-after sharp edges. I am aware, however, that not everyone has easy access to these pastes so I have included the two-piece method as an alternative.

Before covering your stacked buttercreamed or ganached cake, place it on a spare cake board that has been covered in waxed paper.

ALL-IN-ONE SHARP EDGES: USING SUGARPASTE (FONDANT) WITH ADDED GUM

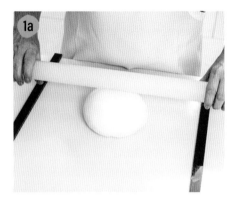

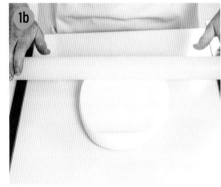

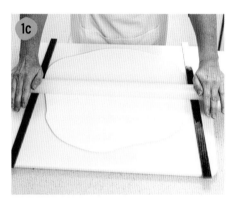

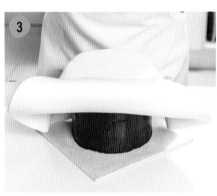

Tip

Smear vegetable fat on your rolling surface rather than sprinkling the surface with icing sugar as icing sugar can dry out and can mark the underside of your sugarpaste (fondant).

1. Knead the sugarpaste until warm and pliable. Place it on a surface that has been lightly smeared with white vegetable fat (shortening). Roll out the paste to a depth of 5mm (³⁄₁₆in). It is a good idea to use 5mm-deep spacers for this, as these ensure an even thickness.

2. Drape the paste over a rolling pin and lift it carefully over the cake.

3. Position the paste centrally over the cake and smooth the top surface of the cake, to remove any lumps and bumps, using a smoother. Smooth the top edge using the palm of your hand. Always make sure your hands are clean and dry with no traces of cake crumbs before smoothing sugarpaste.

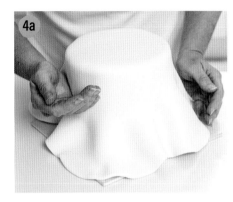

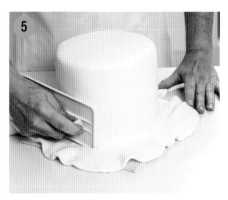

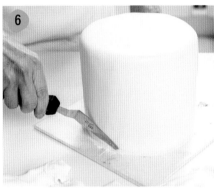

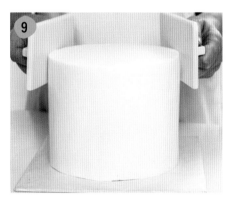

4. Using your cupped hands in an upwards movement, encourage the sugarpaste onto the sides of the cake to adjust to the shape of your cake. Do not press down on any pleats in the paste; instead, open them out and redistribute the paste until the cake is completely covered.

5. Smooth the sides using a smoother. While pressing down with the smoother, run the flat edge around the base of the cake to create a cutting line.

6. Trim away the excess paste with a palette knife to create a neat edge.

7. Take another cake board covered with waxed paper and place it on top of your covered cake. Using two hands flip the boards over so that the cake rests on its top.

8. Working quickly, take your smoother and gently stroke the paste down towards the board to turn your curved cake top into a sharp edge. This does take a little practice, so if you are finding your icing is starting to dry, simply use the heat of your hand to warm it up a little. I find it best to work on the edge in stages, so I go around the whole cake to achieve an approximate edge and then go around again to perfect.

9. Once you are happy with the finish, turn your cake the right way up and remove the top board. Finally, with two smoothers, adjust and polish the icing as much as required.

TWO-PIECE SHARP EDGES – USING STANDARD SUGARPASTE (FONDANT)

This is an easy technique for creating very sharp edges, but, as two pieces of paste are used, there will be a join. Think carefully whether it is better to have the join on the side or the top of the cake. For example, on the *Puffy the Puffin* cake (on pages 102–111), the join is on the side as it is covered by the sea decoration; consequently, the sides are covered first, followed by the top.

Place your buttercreamed or ganached cake on a cake board the same size as the cake. Knead the sugarpaste (fondant) until warm. Then roll the paste into a long sausage shape with its length equalling the circumference of the cake. Place the sausage on your work surface and roll over it to widen the paste to at least the height of the cake and thin to a thickness of 5mm (³⁄₁₆in).

The sides

1. Turn the paste over and cut it into a rectangle slightly larger than both the circumference and the height of your cake. Position the cake on its side on the paste so that the top is flush with one long edge.

2. Roll the cake up in the sugarpaste. Trim the paste as necessary to create a neat, straight join and rub the join closed using the heat of your hand: remember that the join is often disguised by the decoration.

3. Finally, with a palette knife, cut away the excess from the base, then stand the cake upright.

The top

1. Roll out more sugarpaste and use it to cover the top.

2. Place a board covered in waxed paper over the top and invert the cake. Then, with a palette knife, carefully trim away the excess sugarpaste.

3. Turn the cake back over, remove the waxed paper and smooth the top and sides.

COVERING BOARDS

There are many different ways of covering cake boards. In this book I've used the same method throughout to save on paste and keep things simpler. If you prefer to use another method, be my guest!

Tip

For larger cakes, you will need to do this in two stages.

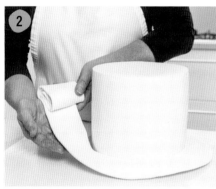

1. Place your covered cake centrally on the cake board. Using 5mm (³⁄₁₆in) spacers, roll out some sugarpaste into a long strip, long enough to fit around your cake board. Cut one straight edge using a palette knife.

2. Brush the cake board with cooled boiled water. Then, with the cut edge abutting your covered cake, position the paste strip on the cake board.

3. Using a smoother, ensure that the sugarpaste abuts the cake snugly. Cut to fit and blend the join with the heat of your hand.

4. Cut away the excess from the edge of the board using a palette knife, as shown.

COLOURING UP

COLOURING SUGARPASTE (FONDANT) AND MODELLING PASTE

Sugarpaste (fondant) and modelling paste are available commercially in all kinds of colours. However, if you can't find the exact shade you are searching for, or if only a small amount of colour is required, it is often best to colour your own paste or adjust the colour of a commercial paste.

Colouring sugarpaste (fondant) can be a very sticky and messy process, so before you begin, rub your hands with white vegetable fat to help prevent your skin taking on the paste colour. Keep an old-fashioned bar of soap to hand, with which to wash your hands afterwards.

PASTEL COLOURS

1. If you want to colour only a small amount of paste, or you wish to make a pastel colour, place a little paste colour (not liquid colour) on the end of a cocktail stick or toothpick and add it to your sugarpaste.

2. Knead the colour into the paste.

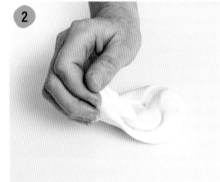

STRONG/VIBRANT COLOURS

1. If you wish to create a deep rich colour, add a larger amount of paste colour to the end of a palette knife and add to the paste.

2. Knead the paste to distribute the colour; initially it will look streaky (a), but as you continue to knead the colour will become uniform (b). Add more paste colour as necessary to achieve a deeper colour. If the sugarpaste becomes really sticky, due to the amount of paste colour used, add a pinch of gum to firm it up a little and leave to rest.

White plus two shades of green, both made using the same paste colour in different proportions.

BLENDING/MIXING COLOURS

If you wish to change the colour of sugarpaste that is already coloured, it is much easier to knead in another coloured sugarpaste than try to change the colour by adding paste colour. By doing so you should feel more in control and less likely to make wasteful mistakes.

Once you are happy with your chosen colour, pop it into an airtight plastic bag and place to one side.

Tip

If you wish to colour large amounts of sugarpaste (fondant), it is easier to colour a smaller amount of sugarpaste a shade darker than you require, then gradually add this into a larger amount of white, than to try to colour the paste all in one go.

COLOUR VARIABLES

Some variables can affect the colours that you mix. These include the following:

Time: Colours often darken over time so, if possible, leave your paste to rest for a few hours before using it. This way, you won't have to add as much colour.

Ingredients: White vegetable fat, margarine and butter all make colours turn darker. Lemon juice, on the other hand, softens colours.

Light: Some colours, especially pinks, purple and blues, can fade in bright light so it is important that you protect your paste and finished creations from direct sunlight.

COLOURING MODELLING CHOCOLATE

Warm up your white modelling chocolate by placing it in a microwave for a few seconds. Pull off a piece, roll a ball, then make a well in the centre with your thumb.

Add some edible food dust to the well in the modelling chocolate, then carefully knead in until the colour is even. Add more colour if required.

Remember that to obtain certain colours you may need to add white food dust to disguise the creamy base colour.

Tip

Make sure you are using food dust colours and not coloured chalks. Throughout this book, I have been using Rainbow Dust powder colours, which work beautifully.

Useful mixing tips

- Allow time: Don't underestimate how long it takes to mix colours that blend and harmonize.
- Mix colours in daylight: Always try to work in daylight when selecting and mixing your colours, to give the most accurate results.
- Start with sugarpaste (fondant): It is much easier to mix colours into sugarpaste (fondant) than modelling paste, so mix the colour you require first before adding the gum to make modelling paste.
- Add dark to light: It takes only a little of a dark colour to change a light colour, but it takes much more of a light colour to change a dark colour.
- Use single pigments: For the brightest, most intense colours, use colours made from one pigment only; check the label of your paste colours to see how many pigments the paste contains.
- Use tints, not white: A tint may look white when placed with other colours on your cake, but it will be much more pleasing on the eye than a stark, true white.
- Blending colours: One trick I often use is to add a little of one colour into another to change it fractionally, so that the two colours are more in harmony with one another.

ADDING COLOUR TO AN AIRBRUSH

Using an edible colour designed for airbrushes, carefully squeeze out the required amount of colour into the inkwell on top of the airbrush.

STORAGE AND TRANSPORTATION

The following conditions will adversely affect your decorated cake:
- Sunlight will fade and alter the colours of icing, so always store in a dark place.
- Humidity can have a disastrous effect on decorations, causing the icing to become soft and to wilt if free-standing. It can also cause dark colours to bleed into lighter colours.
- Heat can melt icing, especially buttercream, and prevent the sugarpaste (fondant) crusting over.

It is, therefore, best to protect your decorated cake as much as possible. Store your completed cake in a clean, covered cardboard cake box and place somewhere cool and dry, not in a fridge. If the box is slightly larger than the cake and the cake is to be transported, use non-slip matting to prevent the cake moving. If the weather is humid, use a dehumidifier and transport it in an air-conditioned vehicle, if possible.

WELCOME HOME

Here is a perfect cake to welcome someone back home after they've been away for a while; to give to a couple setting up their first home, or even as a moving-house cake. 'Home is where the heart is': our homes are very important to us, so let's celebrate them!

THE INSPIRATION

Cheerful colourful Caribbean homes seen on my recent travels and an artist friend's painting of the Crooked House (*Krzywy Domek*) in Sopot, Poland were my starting points for this design. Further research led me to discover vibrant, fun folk art paintings from around the world: paintings by the Portuguese artist Miguel Freitas particularly caught my eye. Freitas's wonky houses and street scenes play with perspective and look so appealing. Going with the concept of buildings with no verticals or horizontals, I've created my own colourful street scene with a cozy home at the heart.

Here are just some of the colourful buildings seen across the globe, which have inspired this cake:

1. San Juan, Puerto Rico;

2. Philipsburg, St Maarten;

3. Santa Marta, Columbia.

Mix up your house designs as much as you wish.

Experiment with colour combinations.

Remember, with these houses, nothing needs to be straight, horizontal or vertical!

YOU WILL NEED

MATERIALS

- Cake – 12.5cm (5in) diameter × 15cm (6in) height – baked in two halves
- 1kg (2¼lb) white sugarpaste (fondant) – use 800g (1¾lb) to cover the cake
- CMC/Tylose/gum – if using soft sugarpaste (fondant) or working in humid conditions
- Buttercream or chocolate ganache to add as a base coat before the sugarpaste (fondant)
- Edible food dusts: a selection of colours including white
- Cocoa butter
- White vegetable fat
- Sugar glue (see page 17)

EQUIPMENT AND TOOLS

- 20cm (8in) cake board
- Waxed paper/tracing paper
- Pencil and eraser
- Cutting wheel
- Dresden tool
- Scissors
- Rolling pin
- Palette knife
- No.s 2 and 17 piping tubes (by PME)
- Small ball tool
- Selection of paintbrushes
- White plates or paint palettes
- Source of heat – simmering pan of hot water or a tea-light in a pot warmer
- Sugar shaper (sugar extruder) and assorted discs
- 15mm (⁹⁄₁₆in) sand-coloured ribbon
- Non-toxic glue stick

PREPARING THE CAKE

Level, stack and cover your baked cakes with white sugarpaste (fondant) to create one 15cm (6in) tall cake with sharp edges, following the instructions in the Techniques section (see pages 22–24).

Allow the icing to dry, then place centrally on the 20cm (8in) cake board.

1. Individually, place some light blue and white food dust on one side of a white plate, then add a little cocoa butter on the other side. Position the plate over a source of heat: you can use either a simmering pan of water or, if more convenient, a tea-light in a pot warmer or suitable container. Once the gentle heat has begun to melt the cocoa butter, mix a little into the coloured dusts to create a paint.

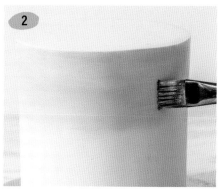

2. Load a large, flat brush with the mixed paint and apply with horizontal sweeping strokes to the top third of the cake for the sky. Keep the paint mix fairly dry to give a light, feathery finish to your strokes.

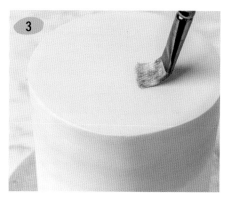

3. Paint the top of the cake to complete the sky.

CREATING THE HOUSES

Measure the diameter of your cake. Then cut a piece of waxed or tracing paper the same length plus 1cm (⅜in) overlap × 18cm (7in) high. You can use my finished cake designs as reference or have a go at creating your own. Either way, start by sketching the focal-point home in the centre of your paper using a pencil. Then add three homes either side. Fill up the paper strip but leave the overlap blank.

Roll out white sugarpaste (fondant) 2–3mm (¹⁄₁₆–⅛in) thick and large enough to create one house.

> ### Tip
>
> If you are using a soft sugarpaste (fondant) or working in humid conditions, you will probably need to add a little CMC/Tylose/gum to strengthen the paste to prevent the houses distorting when you lift them.

1. Place the template over the rolled-out paste. Take a cutting wheel and roll the large end firmly around the outline of a house, its windows, door and roof. You are aiming to indent the paste to create cutting lines so check that you have pressed firmly enough before removing the template completely.

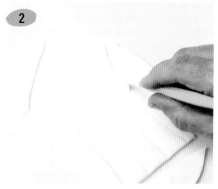

2. Still using the larger cutting wheel, cut around the outline of the house, making sure that you cut all the way through the paste. Remove the excess paste.

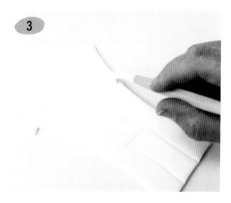

3. Using the small end of the cutting wheel, emboss the roof line, door and windows, paying particular attention to the corners. It is better if the lines are slightly too short than too long.

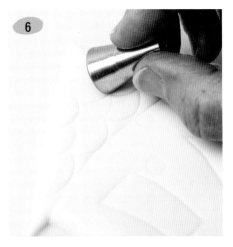

4. Next, smooth and round the walls of the house, using the heat of a finger.

5. Emboss circles at random onto the front of the house using the no. 17 piping tube.

6. Create roof tiles by holding the wider end of the piping tube at an angle and embossing half-moons. You will need to roll the piping tube gently backwards and forwards to create the curve. Create the bottom line of roof tiles first, then work upwards.

7. Dampen the surface of the cake where the house is to be positioned with a little water. Then carefully lift your sugar house and position it.

8. Create all but the last house in the same way, varying the roof finishes – for example, create small tiles by indenting the paste with the narrow end of a piping tube. To do this, hold the tube at an angle and emboss overlapping tiles from the ridge of the roof downwards.

9. Attach the houses to the side of the cake, leaving a small gap between each house.

10. Rub over the join to smooth the paste using a finger, then tidy up the gap by running a dresden tool down the join. To make sure that the last house fits, place the template back on the cake and make any necessary adjustments to the shape outline. Create and attach.

ADDING THE DETAILS

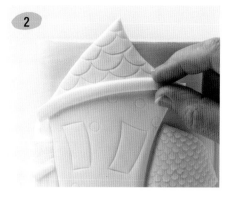

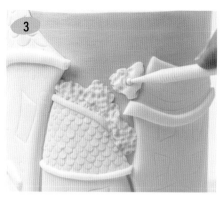

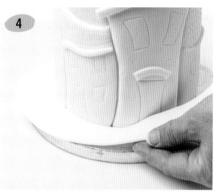

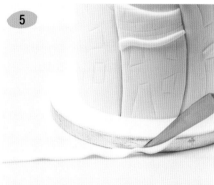

1. Using the finished cake photographs to guide you (see pages 29, 30 and 37), cut strips from rolled-out sugarpaste for roof ridges, fascias and door headers. Attach in place and trim to fit using scissors.

2. Stroke the cut edges of these strips with your fingers to curve and smooth.

3. To create the trees and shrubs, tear off small prices of sugarpaste and attach to the cake. Take a small ball tool and press into this paste to create a textured finish.

4. For the cobbled path, firstly roll out a thin strip of sugarpaste. Cut one edge straight, then attach around the board as shown.

5. Cut the edge flush with the board using a palette knife.

6. Add a step in front of the main front door and a large threshold stone using a flattened ball of sugarpaste. Press the edges of the stone to meet the board.

7. To create the cobblestones, roll balls of sugarpaste in a variety of sizes. Dampen the sugarpaste path, leaving the area in front of the main house dry. Place the balls of paste onto the path, then, using a dry brush, move them around to eliminate as many gaps as possible. Next, press down gently using a finger to flatten the tops of the balls and to encourage an even better fit.

8. To fill the gaps between the cobbles, you can use either sugarpaste mixed with water to a paint-like consistency or very soft royal icing – royal icing will dry more quickly. Using a flat-headed brush, spread the mixture you are using over a section of cobbles. Then, using a wet brush, go over the area to remove most of the paste and reveal the tops of the cobbles.

PAINTING THE HOUSES

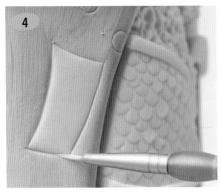

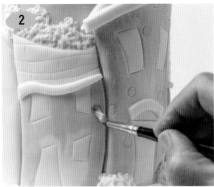

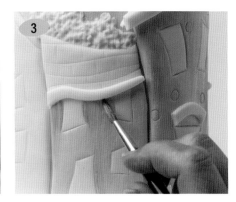

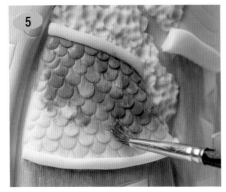

1. Choose a house to paint. I suggest that you start at the back of the cake so that by the time you reach the front you are feeling confident. Choose or mix two or three shades of coloured dusts. Place these shades on the edge of a white plate and add some cocoa butter. Position the plate over a source of heat; once the cocoa butter has melted, mix a little into the dust colours to create a thick paint.

2. Using vertical strokes, paint over the walls of your chosen house with the lightest of your colours, taking care not to paint over the windows and door. However, if you do, simply take a clean paintbrush, dip it in the melted cocoa butter and brush away your mistake.

3. Next, add the darker colour under the roof and perhaps down one side of the building. Use a dry brush to blend the colours as you paint. The beauty of cocoa painting is that you can keep adding colour on top of colour until you are happy with the result.

4. Once the walls are complete, take a thin brush and carefully touch up the indented recesses around the windows and door.

5. To paint the small tiles on the orange house, mix up shades of one colour. Then paint sections of each colour at random over the roof, blending the colours into each other as you go until the roof is completely covered.

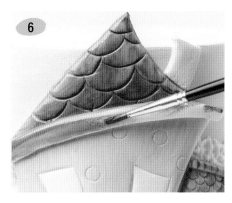

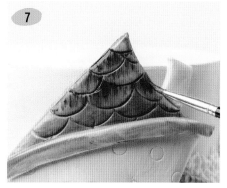

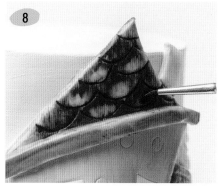

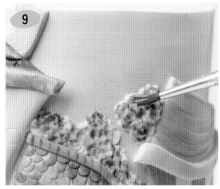

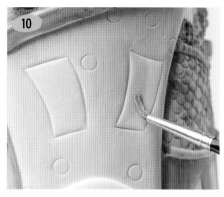

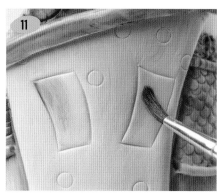

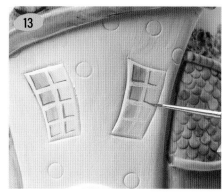

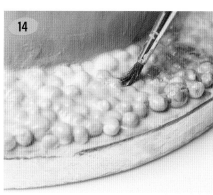

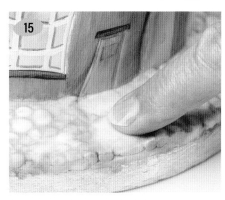

6. To create the paint effect on the pink roof tiles on the yellow house, first paint the roof all over with a mid-pink colour.

7. Next, add dark pink lines emanating from the top of each tile as shown.

8. To complete, take a clean brush, dip it into the melted cocoa butter and make upward strokes from the lower edge of each tile to remove some of the paint. Paint the remaining roofs in your choice of colours and styles.

9. To paint the trees and shrubs, mix a selection of different green food dusts with cocoa butter, then apply each colour in sections, blending the colours as you go.

10. To paint the windows, start by applying a base coat of light blue in vertical strokes.

11. Next, take a dry brush and dip it into some bright blue dust. Knock off the excess on the side of the plate. Using vertical sweeping strokes, brush over approximately one-third of the painted light blue window.

12. Mix up some white paint; using a thin brush, paint the window frames and glazing bars.

13. Take a very fine brush such as a no. 0000 and paint blue 'L' shapes to help define each pane of glass. Repeat the process for the remaining window.

14. For the cobblestones, mix up a selection of creams, oranges and pinks, then paint over all the cobbles, blending and changing the colours.

15. Allow the painted cobbles to dry. Then, using a finger, rub over the tops of the cobbles to melt and remove some of the paint. You are aiming to reveal some, but not all, of the white sugarpaste beneath the paint.

FINISHING TOUCHES

1. To adjust the sky colour if required, add a subtle touch of pale purple to the blue. Then add clouds using white as seen in the finished photographs of the cake on pages 29, 30 and 37, opposite.

2. To create the railing along the front of the orange house, warm up some white sugarpaste that has had a little gum added to it by kneading. Next, add some white vegetable fat to stop the paste getting sticky and dip the paste in cooled boiled water to soften it. You are looking for a paste with the consistency of chewed chewing gum! Place the softened paste into the barrel of the sugar shaper and the no. 2 piping tube into the top, and screw together. Pump the shaper until the pressure has built up and the paste begins to flow easily from the tube. Squeeze out lengths onto your work board, guiding the paste into the required shape as shown. Adjust the shape of each by using a dresden tool to pull each loop taut. Squeeze out two additional straight lengths. Allow the paste to firm up. Next, use a palette knife to cut the loops so that they are all the same length, then attach them in place on the cake using a little sugar glue.

3. Add the horizontal bars as shown on the finished cake, above. Finally, add a sand-coloured ribbon to the edge of the cake drum using a non-toxic glue stick.

The finished cake.

HEART DESIGN

A heart – the universal symbol of love – makes the perfect
motif for a cake celebrating an anniversary, Valentine's Day
or Mothering Sunday.

'The best and most beautiful things in the world cannot be
seen nor even touched, but just felt in the heart.'
– Helen Keller (1880–1968)

THE INSPIRATION

I never know when inspiration will strike – sometimes it comes completely
unexpectedly. A good neighbour of mine persuaded me to join her at what
she thought was a card-making demonstration. It turned out, however, to be a
have-a-go-at-iris-folding session. Iris folding is a distinctive, spiralling papercraft
technique. As with many things, once you know how, it is a relatively easy
technique that works beautifully with paper, ribbon and fabric – would it work
in sugar?
Feeling inspired, I tried at least three different approaches before I had to admit
to myself that it simply didn't work, at least not in a way that I was happy with.
I compromised and designed a heart that gives a nod to the spiralling patterns of
iris folding but is easy to replicate in sugar.

1. *Detail on the Karni Mata temple, Deshnoke, India;*
2. *My own iris-folding pattern made from ribbon;*
3. *Iris motif seen on the lino floor of the Chinatown
   Heritage Centre, Singapore.*

YOU WILL NEED

MATERIALS

- Cake – 15cm (6in) diameter × 15cm (6in)
- 900g (2lb) peach sugarpaste (fondant)
- Buttercream or chocolate ganache to add as a base coat before the sugarpaste (fondant)
- Modelling paste: 175g (6oz) purple, 15g (½oz) red, 10g (⅜oz) orange, 15g (½oz) peach, 15g (½oz) pink, 15g (½oz) white, 15g (½oz) pale orange
- Edible food dusts – shades of orange, peach, pink and red
- White vegetable fat
- Sugar glue (see page 17)

EQUIPMENT AND TOOLS

- Paper for templates
- 18cm (7in) waxed paper circle
- 18cm (7in) or larger cake board covered in waxed paper
- Letter stamps, e.g. Sweet Sticks (by Sweet Stamp)
- Sticky pad (by Sweet Stamp)
- Smoother
- Mini message embossers (by Sweet Stamp)
- Glass-headed dressmakers' pins
- Two A4 – 297 x 210mm (11¾ x 8¼in) – plastic document wallets
- 20cm (8in) cake board
- 1mm- (1⁄16in-) deep spacers
- Cutters similar to:
  - 7cm (2¾in) circle cutter
  - 65mm (2½in) petunia cutter (by FMM)
  - 50mm (2in) five-petal blossom cutter (by PME)
  - 30mm (1¼in) scalloped circle cutter (by PME)
  - 20mm (¾in) eight-petal daisy cutter (by PME)
  - 10mm (⅜in) teardrop cutter (by Lindy's Cakes)
  - No.s 4 and 17 piping tubes (by PME)
  - 25mm (1in) heart cutter (by FMM)
- Blossom embossers (by Patchwork Cutters)
- Leaf embosser (by Patchwork Cutters)
- Cutting wheel
- Dresden tool
- Scissors
- Rolling pin
- Palette knife
- Small ball tool
- Scriber
- Selection of paintbrushes
- White plate or paint palette
- Sugar shaper (sugar extruder) and assorted discs
- Narrow ribbon to cover the edge of the board
- Non-toxic glue stick

PREPARING AND EMBOSSING THE CAKE

Cut paper into strips to make placement templates. You will need strips of the following heights: 3.5cm (1⅜in), 6.5cm (2½in), 9.5cm (3¾in) and 12cm (4¾in).

Level, stack and cover your baked cakes with peach sugarpaste (fondant) to create one 15cm (6in) tall cake with sharp edges, following the instructions in the Techniques section (see pages 22–24). Immediately emboss the soft icing with the words for 'love' in different languages: *amore* (Italian), *amor* (Portuguese), *cinta* (Indonesian), *kärlek* (Swedish), *liefde* (Dutch), *Liebe* (German), *láska* (Czech), *cariad* (Welsh), *ljubav* (Bosnian), *amour* (French) and *sevgi* (Azerbaijani) – or use your own text, following the instructions below.

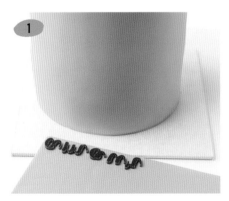

1. To create the lowest line of words, first choose letters and spell out a word on your work surface. Place the sticky pad carefully over the word placing it near but not on the bottom edge of the pad. Lift up the pad and the letters should be attached and be a mirror image of the word.

2. Starting at the beginning of the word, carefully press the letters on the pad into the soft paste. Slowly rock the pad to the right around the cake, so that all the letters are embossed. Use a smoother to flatten the embossed paste as necessary. Continue to add words around the base of the cake, ensuring that you leave sufficient space between each word.

3. For the second row of words, place the 3.5cm-(1⅜in-) high template strip against the cake and the waxed paper circle on top of the cake. Select new letters and carefully press each letter into the soft icing to spell out a word, using a smoother placed on top of the circle of waxed paper to help stabilize the cake as you emboss the letters. Once a word is spelled, remove the letters using the sticky pad or your fingers – you might even find that some fall out of their own accord.

Tip

For letters that are repeated, like the 'a' in *cariad* – the Welsh word for love – you will need to remove the first 'a' before you can emboss the second.

4. Continue up the cake, adding more words using the 6.5cm (2½in), 9.5cm (3¾in) and 12cm (4¾in) placement templates to guide you and the smoother to steady the cake.

5. Create full words using the mini message embossers, by sliding the appropriate letters into the holder. Emboss these in the spaces above and below the larger words until you are happy with the result. Allow the sugarpaste to dry.

PAINTING THE CAKE

1. Using a white plate or paint palette, mix up your chosen dust colours with water to make a thick paint.

2. Load a flat-headed brush and start to paint over the dried embossed icing using sweeping horizontal strokes. Change colours as you paint, blending one colour into another.

3. To help highlight the words, use a fine brush to paint a dark colour inside the letters.

4. Blend in any overpainting of the edges by sweeping a clean flat-headed brush over the words. Continue until you are happy with the finished effect. Finally, paint the top of the cake with concentric circular strokes of colour using the flat-headed brush. Allow to dry.

CREATING THE HEART

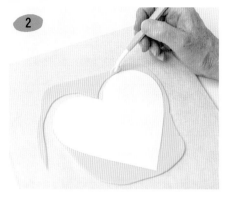

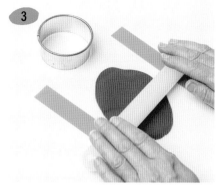

Tip

Use spacers to ensure that your paste pieces are the same uniform thickness.

1. Cut out a 13.5 × 15cm (5¼ × 6in) oblong from white paper, fold in half to make a 13.5 × 7.5cm (5¼ × 3in) oblong. Making sure that the fold of the paper will form the centre of the heart, draw half a heart using the full width and height of the paper. Cut around your outline with scissors. Trace around this shape onto another sheet of white paper and cut it out so that you have two copies.

2. Roll out the remaining peach sugarpaste to a thickness of 2mm (1⁄16in). Place onto your waxed-paper-covered board. Position one of the heart templates over the paste and carefully cut around it with a cutting wheel.

3. Roll out the red modelling paste between narrow spacers and cut out a circle using a twisting motion and the 7cm (2¾in) circle cutter.

4. Carefully place the circle onto the top left-hand section of the heart, taking care not to distort the circle while transferring. Use a smoother to polish and iron out any irregularities in the surface of the circle.

5. Next, thinly roll out the peach modelling paste between 1mm- (1⁄16in-) deep spacers. To achieve a clean, unfeathered cut edge, place the paste over the petunia cutter and roll over it with a small rolling pin. If necessary, rub a finger over the edges of the cutter to help release the paste. Turn over the flower and stick it on top of the red circle using sugar glue.

6. Cut out the purple five-petal blossom, using the same method. Carefully position the flower so that the petals overlap the joins below, as shown.

7. Build up the design by adding a scalloped circle, an eight-petal daisy, a circle cut using the no. 17 piping tube and, finally, five small, white teardrops.

8. To create the first shape that fits snugly around the circle, roll out the pink modelling paste between the 1mm (1⁄16in) spacers. Use the 7cm (2¾in) circle cutter to cut out an almost complete circle, then a cutting wheel to create a tapered triangular shape outside the circle as shown.

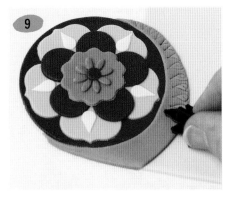

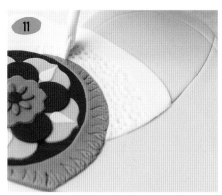

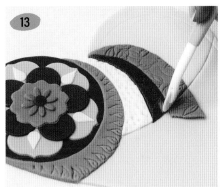

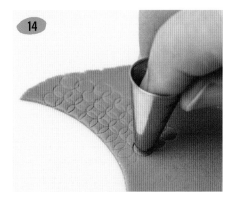

9. Lift the resulting shape and place on the heart, ensuring that it abuts neatly with the red circle. Trim away the excess paste from the top and side of the heart. Next, take a leaf embosser and repeatedly press it into the edge of the tapered pink paste as shown.

10. Roll out the white modelling paste using the 1mm (¹⁄₁₆in) spacers. Cut out a partial circle as before. Add texture to the area outside the circle by embossing the head of a glass-headed dressmakers' pin repeatedly into the soft paste.

11. Place the paste into the heart to the right of the pink tapered strip, referring to the steps for guidance. Use a cutting wheel to cut through the lower edge of the paste, then continue the line to emboss a roughly horizontal curve. This curved line is to help with placement. Remove the excess paste from the top of the heart using a cutting wheel.

12. Cut the textured white paste into a tapered, curved triangle.

13. Continue adding, texturing and cutting different coloured shapes, using the embossed line to guide you.

14. To create the overlapping circular embossed pattern, use the no. 17 PME piping tube as shown.

15. Add radial lines to the outer purple paste by using the edge of the 1mm (¹⁄₁₆in) spacers to emboss the soft paste. Finally, fill the lower section of the heart, repeating the colours and textures.

ATTACHING THE HEART

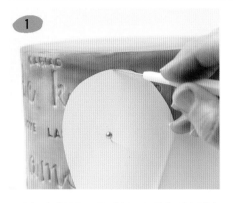

Tip

If paste circles get stuck inside the piping tube at step 6, use a dry paintbrush to push them out.

1. Position your folded heart template at a slight angle onto your painted cake. Experiment with different angles and different positions on your cake until you are happy with the placement. Use glass-headed dressmakers' pins to secure. Take a scriber and scribe around the outline of the heart, making sure that the line is visible. This will help with positioning your completed sugar heart.

2. Paint sugar glue inside the scribed heart and allow it to turn tacky. Meanwhile, remove the waxed paper, with its decorated heart still in place, from the cake board. Then carefully peel away the waxed paper from the back of the decorated heart and position on the cake using the scribed lines to guide you.

3. To neaten the edges of the heart, warm up some red modelling paste by kneading. Next, add some white vegetable fat to stop the paste getting sticky and then dip the paste in cooled boiled water to soften it. Place the softened paste into the barrel of the sugar shaper and the medium round disc into the top and screw together. Pump the shaper until the pressure has built up and the paste begins to be released from the extruder. Squeeze out a length that is long enough to go around half the heart and leave it on your work surface to firm up a little. Swap the disc in the sugar shaper for the smallest circle and squeeze out two more lengths. Then change colour to purple and swap back to the largest circle disc. Squeeze out another length, long enough to go around half the heart.

4. Attach the two thinner lengths to the design as shown, using sugar glue or water. Cut to size. Paint the outer edges of the heart with a little water or sugar glue. Next cut one end of the purple length at an angle and place centrally at the top of the heart. Wrap the length around the left-hand side of the heart. Repeat with the red on the right-hand side. Trim to fit.

5. Cut out a 2.5cm (1in) red heart from modelling paste. Allow it to firm up on your work surface before attaching as desired (see above).

6. To create the white dots, thinly roll out some white modelling paste, then use the no. 4 piping tube to cut out white circles. Do this by pressing and twisting the tube into the paste.

7. Attach to your heart design using a damp paintbrush.

FINISHING TOUCHES

Place your decorated cake centrally onto the 20cm (8in) cake board.

Roll out the remaining purple modelling paste into a long strip, long enough to fit around your cake board. Cut one edge straight. Starting at the back of your cake, with the cut edge abutting your decorated cake, position the paste strip around the cake board. Cut to fit and blend the join with the heat of your hand. Cut away the excess from the edge of the board using a palette knife.

Finally, attach a suitable ribbon to the edge of your board using a non-toxic glue stick.

DANCING IN THE RAIN

This is a unique cake that celebrates friendship, achievement
in the face of adversity and shared experiences.
After all: 'life isn't about waiting for the storm to pass…
It's about learning to dance in the rain.'
– Vivian Greene, author, artist and speaker

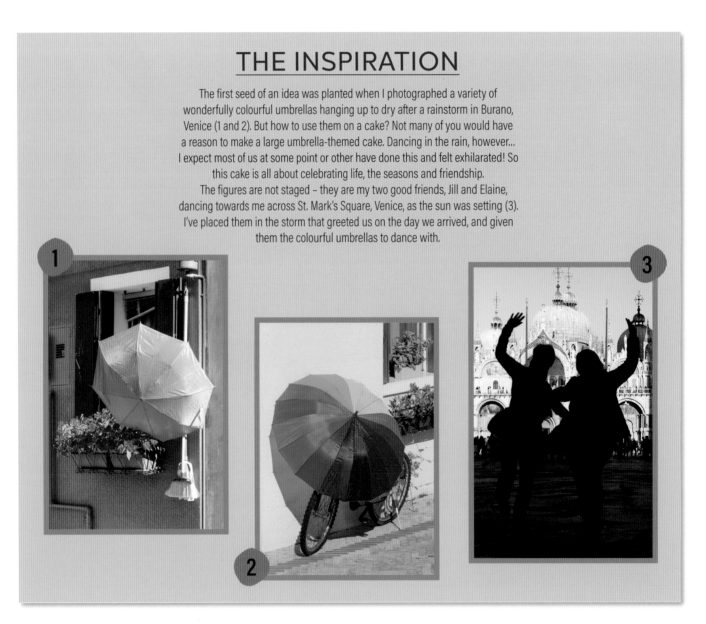

THE INSPIRATION

The first seed of an idea was planted when I photographed a variety of
wonderfully colourful umbrellas hanging up to dry after a rainstorm in Burano,
Venice (1 and 2). But how to use them on a cake? Not many of you would have
a reason to make a large umbrella-themed cake. Dancing in the rain, however…
I expect most of us at some point or other have done this and felt exhilarated! So
this cake is all about celebrating life, the seasons and friendship.
The figures are not staged – they are my two good friends, Jill and Elaine,
dancing towards me across St. Mark's Square, Venice, as the sun was setting (3).
I've placed them in the storm that greeted us on the day we arrived, and given
them the colourful umbrellas to dance with.

YOU WILL NEED

MATERIALS

- Cake – 12.5cm (5in) diameter × 20cm (8in) height. I recommend that you bake three layers
- 1kg (2¼lb) white sugarpaste (fondant)
- Buttercream or chocolate ganache to add as a base coat before the sugarpaste (fondant)
- Modelling paste: 25g (⅞oz) mid-blue, 25g (⅞oz) navy blue, 25g (⅞oz) emerald green, 5g (⅛oz) lime green, 5g (⅛oz) jade green, 25g (⅞oz) purple, 10g (⅜oz) pink, 25g (⅞oz) red, 10g (⅜oz) white, 5g (⅛oz) yellow, 5g (⅛oz) orange, 10g (⅜oz) grey, 10g (⅜oz) brown, 15g (½oz) flesh, 5g (⅛oz) black

- Edible food dusts: black, white, pink, blue, brown
- Cocoa butter
- White vegetable fat
- Sugar glue (see page 17)
- Piping gel

EQUIPMENT AND TOOLS

- Template (see page 136)
- Two A4 – 297 x 210mm (11¾ x 8¼in) – plastic document wallets
- 18cm (7in) cake board
- Waxed paper/tracing paper
- Pencil and eraser
- Cutting wheel
- Dresden tool

- Scissors
- Rolling pin
- Palette knife
- No.s 1 and 18 piping tubes (by PME)
- Small ball tool
- Selection of paintbrushes
- White plate
- Source of heat – simmering pan of hot water or a tea-light in a pot warmer
- Sugar shaper (sugar extruder) and assorted discs
- Narrow ribbon to cover the edge of the board
- Non-toxic glue stick

PREPARING AND PAINTING THE CAKE

Level, stack and cover your baked cakes with white sugarpaste (fondant), to create one 20cm (8in) tall cake with sharp edges, following instructions in the Techniques section (see pages 22–24).

Allow the icing to dry, then place the cake centrally on the 18cm (7in) cake board. Cover the cake board with a strip of rolled-out sugarpaste (fondant), trim to size and blend the join with the heat of a finger.

1. Individually, place some black and white food dust to one side of a white plate, then add some cocoa butter. Position the plate over a source of heat. You can either use a simmering pan of water or a tea-light in a pot warmer or suitable container. Once the gentle heat has begun to melt the cocoa butter, mix a little into the coloured dusts to create a paint.

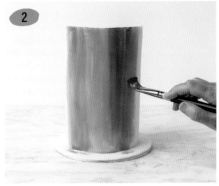

2. Load a large, flat brush with the mixed paint and apply with vertical sweeping strokes to the sides of the cake, changing and blending the colours as you go. Keep the paint mix fairly dry to give a light feathery finish to the strokes.

3. Once you have painted the base coat, load a brush with white paint and add sweeping vertical strokes to the front of the cake, leaving the base coat showing at the top and lower edges. This creates the area where the figures dance.

4. Next load a clean brush with black paint and add short dark strokes above the white to help highlight the front area of the cake. Then paint the cake board with a mix of grey paints, using long sweeping strokes.

5. Working on the back of the cake first, paint horizontal black lines to denote the subtle pavement area.

6. Then take a dry brush and quickly blend each line. Repeat for the sides and front of the cake.

7. Add criss-crosses in black paint to denote pavement slabs.

8. With a dry brush, blend the lines so that they are not so prominent.

9. Next, paint white rain onto the cake using a thin brush and short sweeping strokes at an angle to the vertical. Add a few white puddles to the pavement area and board.

10. Paint the top of the cake using circular strokes as shown.

11. Once you are happy with your painted cake, paint the edges of the cake board grey.

CREATING THE FIRST BAS-RELIEF FIGURE

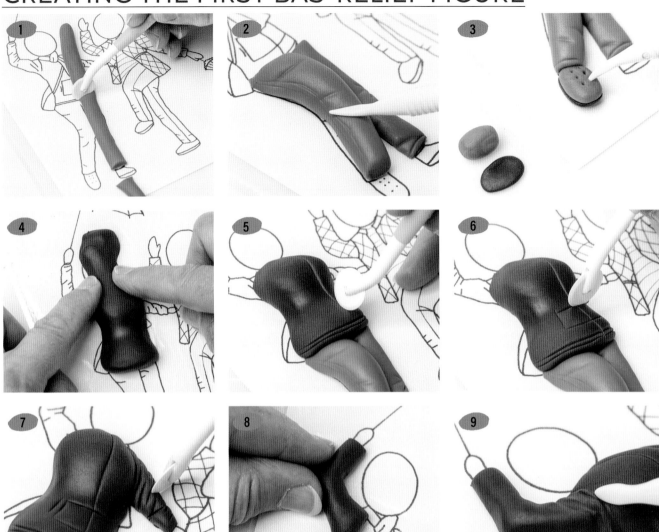

Both of the figures on this cake have been created using a bas-relief technique to give a three-dimensional feel to the design.

1. Copy the template at the back of the book (see page 136) twice and place each copy into a separate plastic document wallet. Knead the mid-blue modelling paste to warm, then roll half into a long sausage to the width of the left-hand figure's left leg. Using a cutting wheel, cut the leg to size as shown, using the template as a guide.

2. Roll a slightly thicker tapered sausage to fit the right leg. Position so that the knee is bent and sits proud of the left leg. Next, add creases into the trousers by pressing a dresden tool into the soft paste as shown. Add seams, using a cutting wheel, down the side of the right leg and along the lower edge of each trouser leg.

3. Roll two small balls of jade green paste, elongating each into a short sausage as shown. Flatten and elongate two small balls of dark navy paste to create the soles. Attach the soles to the base of each shoe. Put the right-hand shoe in place but set the left-hand shoe temporarily to one side. Add six lace eyelets to each shoe using the pointed end of a dresden tool.

4. For the purple coat, roll the purple paste into a sausage the width of the coat template. Thin the waist using your fingers to add shape. Then create the shoulders by stroking the paste upwards with your fingers so that the paste fits the outline of the template. Cut off the excess with a palette knife.

5. Indent a line down the front of the jacket for the zipper, using a cutting wheel.

6. Use the cutting wheel to indent a double hemline and front pocket.

7. For the figure's left arm, roll a small tapered sausage, using the template as a guide. Cut to size with a palette knife and attach in place on the body. Use the cutting wheel to emboss folds in the fabric.

8. Roll a tapered purple sausage to fit the right arm template. Cut to fit, then pinch the elbow to shape.

9. Blend the join between the arm and the jacket body by running a dresden tool through the soft paste to create folds. Continue these up the arm to add more texture to the jacket.

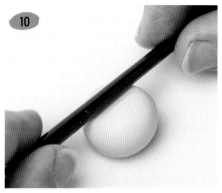

10

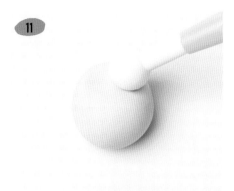

11

12

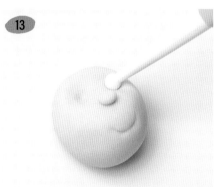

13

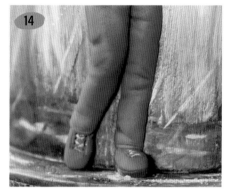

14

15

16

17

Applying more hair to the figure.

10. For the head, take 5g (⅛oz) of flesh-coloured modelling paste. Roll it into a smooth ball with no cracks. Gently roll a small paintbrush over the top third of the ball to flatten the eye area slightly.

11. Using the larger end of a ball tool, indent two shallow circles for the eye area, then add a small button nose.

12. Hold the no. 18 piping tube at an angle and press into the paste, gently rocking the tube from side to side to create a happy smile.

13. Add eye sockets by pressing the small end of the ball tool into the eye area, making sure that they are more or less symmetrically placed. Then roll two small balls of white modelling paste and stick inside each socket using a little water.

14. Using sugar glue, stick your modelled person in place on the cake so that the tip of the right-hand shoe rests on the board. Add the left-hand shoe pointing out away from the cake surface.

15. Create the lime green bag using the template as a guide and add the cross-body strap. Next, roll a thin oblong of pink modelling paste. Ruche it up and drape around the figure's neck to form a scarf.

16. Use a dresden tool to add folds to the scarf as desired. Then add a small section of pink paste to complete the knot in the scarf.

17. To create the hair, firstly warm up some grey-coloured modelling paste by kneading. Next, add some white vegetable fat to stop the paste getting sticky and then dip the paste in cooled boiled water to soften it. Place the softened paste into the barrel of the sugar shaper and the small mesh disc into the top, and screw together. Pump the shaper until the pressure has built up and the paste begins to be released from the extruder. Squeeze out short lengths. Remove these with a dresden tool and attach to your figure to create a hairstyle, using sugar glue or water to stick in place.

CREATING THE OPEN UMBRELLA

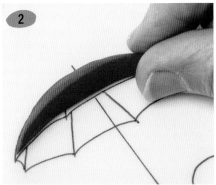

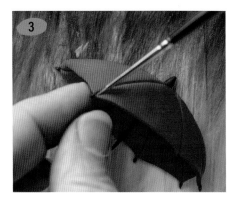

1. For the umbrella, cut out the umbrella template with a pair of scissors. Then, roll out some thin red modelling paste. Place the template on top of the paste and cut around it with a cutting wheel. Run a cutting wheel over the ribs and shaft sections of the umbrella, then remove the template. Go over each of the indented ribs to define them clearly.

2. To make a former to allow the umbrella canopy to stand proud of the cake surface, start by rolling a sausage of red paste. Place the sausage on the umbrella template. Trim and stroke the paste to shape using a palette knife and the heat of your fingers, referring to the photograph for guidance. Once complete, stick in place onto the red cut-out umbrella. To complete the canopy of the umbrella,

use the template to cut out the front canopy section. Mark the ribs as before, then position over the paste former, stretching and easing the paste slightly to encourage it to fit. Use a cutting wheel to trim and tidy the edges of the canopy where the paste meets the template. To make the umbrella shaft, use the sugar shaper and the no. 1 piping tube (rather than a disc). Start by softening some black modelling using white vegetable fat and water, as for the hair. Insert into the sugar shaper fitted with the tube. Squeeze out a suitable length and allow to firm up on your work surface.

3. Meanwhile, using the template, mark the position of the umbrella and its handle with small pinpricks on the cake. Using these as a reference, position the umbrella on the cake. Next, stick the umbrella shaft in position using sugar glue. Add small pieces of black paste for the tips of the umbrella and the top spike.

4. To create the first figure's hands, roll two small ball of flesh-coloured modelling paste. Pinch one side of each ball to create a palm and roll the other side to create wrists. Use scissors to remove a triangle of paste from the palm to create a thumb.

5. Shape the hands into natural positions and attach one to each arm, curling the right-hand hand around the umbrella handle.

CREATING THE SECOND FIGURE

Model the second figure as for the first, using the template on page 136 and suggested modelling paste colours. To create the horizontal stripes for the stripy tee-shirt, roll out yellow paste very thinly and cut narrow strips. Allow them to firm up a little before sticking them in position on the body. Cut to size as required.

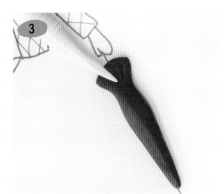

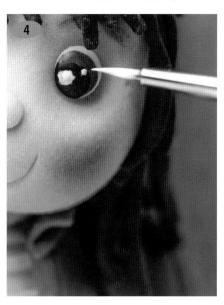

1. Create the green jacket using the template to guide you. Add the criss-cross stitching using a cutting wheel before adding the pieces to the figure.

2. As this figure isn't wearing a scarf, add a small ball of flesh-coloured paste for a neck and shape it using a dresden tool.

3. For the closed umbrella, roll and shape a sausage of orange paste to fit the template. Add folds to the top and body of the umbrella pressing the dresden tool into the soft paste. Add a pink tie. Then add a small ball of pink paste to the base of the umbrella and texture it with the end of the dresden tool. Make a handle and hands as before.

4. To add a little colour to the figures' cheeks, dip a clean, dry paintbrush into the pink food dust. Knock off the excess dust by dabbing the brush onto kitchen paper. Then lightly dust each cheek. Paint the eyes by mixing suitable colours with cocoa butter and paint the irises, pupils and light spots.

FINISHING TOUCHES

Heat piping gel in a microwave for a few seconds until it is warm and smooth; alternatively, heat in a bowl over a pan of simmering water. With a paintbrush, add small droplets of gel to the umbrella and sides of the cake for raindrops. Then create piping gel puddles on the board.

Finally, add a thin ribbon or braid to the edges of the cake board using a non-toxic glue stick.

DANDELION CLOCK

Birthdays mark the passage of time; dandelions change from
suns to moons. Make a wish, tell the time; mark
a special birthday with this delightful design!

'Dandelions, like all things in nature, are beautiful when
you take the time to pay attention to them.'
– June Stoyer, environmental advocate

THE INSPIRATION

At the foot of the Burj Khalifa in Dubai, the world's tallest building, stand fourteen giant stainless-steel dandelion seed heads. I would like to say these were my inspiration for this cake, but in truth, I think they were the catalyst for an idea that was already forming in my mind. Ever since I was a young child I've been fascinated by dandelion clocks, always blowing them to tell the time – I'm sure many of you have too.

When I returned to the UK from Dubai, the hedgerows around me were crammed full of colourful yellow dandelions. Shortly afterwards, I spied a magical field of gossamer dandelion seed heads golden in the late evening sunlight. A few days later they had all but vanished, their delicate puffs having drifted away on the wind. However, the idea had been planted; it was time to design a more permanent reminder of this wonderful wildflower, a flower that innocently entertains generations of children and inspires artists around the globe.

1. One of the giant stainless-steel dandelion sculptures by artist Mirek Struzik (b.1956), next to the Burj Khalifa Dubai;
2. A dandelion growing in my garden!
3. Close-up of a delicate dandelion puff.

YOU WILL NEED

MATERIALS

- Cake – 15cm (6in) diameter × 15cm (6in) height
- 900g (2lb) white sugarpaste (fondant)
- Buttercream or chocolate ganache to add as a base coat before the sugarpaste (fondant)
- Airbrush colours: orange, yellow and peach
- Modelling paste: 5g (⅛oz) dark brown, 20g (¾oz) pale green, 10g (⅜oz) cream
- Flower paste: 20g (¾oz) pale green
- Edible food dusts: a selection of greens, dark blue and white
- White wafer (rice) paper
- White vegetable fat
- Sugar glue (see page 17)
- Orange royal icing: a small amount

EQUIPMENT AND TOOLS

- 20cm (8in) cake board
- Airbrush
- Dandelion leaves or leaf images
- Parachute template (see page 137)
- Wire cutters
- Flat-nose jewellery pliers
- White floristry wire: 24-gauge
- 2cm (¾in) polystyrene ball
- Wooden barbecue skewer
- Cocktail sticks or toothpicks (optional)
- Polystyrene block or cake dummy – to protect parachutes while they dry
- Steam source: steamer or pan of simmering water
- Smoother
- Foam pad
- Waffle foam
- Glass-headed dressmakers' pins
- Craft knife
- Cutting wheel
- Dresden tool
- Veining tool
- Scissors
- Rolling pin
- Ball tool
- Scriber
- Selection of paintbrushes
- White plate or paint palette
- Sugar shaper (sugar extruder) and assorted discs
- Narrow ribbon to cover the edge of the board
- Non-toxic glue stick

PREPARING AND AIRBRUSHING THE CAKE

Level, stack and cover your baked cakes with white sugarpaste (fondant) to create one 15cm (6in) tall cake with sharp edges, following the instructions in the Techniques section (see pages 22–24).

Place your covered cake centrally on the 20cm (8in) cake board. Roll out the remaining white sugarpaste (fondant) into a long strip, long enough to fit around your cake board. Cut one edge straight. With the cut edge abutting your decorated cake, position the paste strip on the cake board. Cut to fit and blend the join with the heat of your hand. Cut away the excess from the edge of the board using a palette knife.

Tip

If you are new to airbrushing, experiment on paper first until you are confident that you can achieve the effect you want.

1. You can either pick dandelion leaves from suitable plants and photograph them or download leaf images from the internet. Resize the leaves to between 8–12.5cm (3⅛–5in) long. Then cut around each leaf outline with a pair of scissors.

2. Fill your airbrush inkwell with peach airbrush colour (see page 27) and apply to your covered cake and board using a circular movement of your hand.

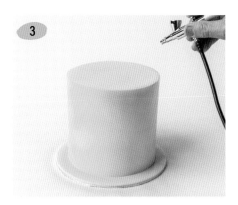

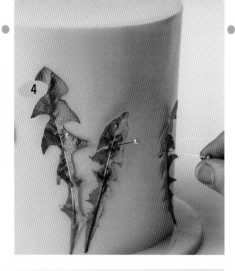

Note
You are not trying to achieve an all-over uniform effect: the paint should be thicker in some places than others.

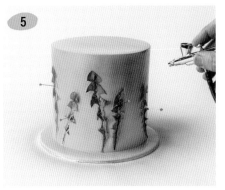

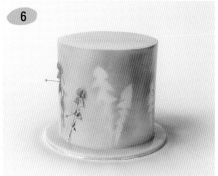

3. On top of this peach, apply some bright yellow colour, again allowing the paint to be thicker in areas. Then tone down the colour a fraction by adding a misting of orange.

4. Pin your cut-out dandelion leaves to the sides of your airbrushed cake using glass-headed pins.

5. Gently spray over the leaves with orange airbrush colour.

6. Then, using the pins, remove the paper leaves and reposition them so that they overlap the first layer of leaves.

7. Arrange the leaves to look as if they are growing in loose clumps. Using the peach airbrush colour, spray over the leaves.

8. Finally, remove all the leaves and allow your airbrushing to dry.

ETCHING THE SEED HEADS

There are two methods for doing this: the method that you choose will depend heavily on the humidity of the environment in which you are working and the time you have available.

When I first created this cake, I used method two. It was a wonderfully hot and dry spell – my sugarpaste (fondant) and airbrushing all dried beautifully. It is my preferred method as the etching is finer and more detailed. However, when I came to remake the cake for the purposes of this book, the humidity was horrendous. My sugarpaste wouldn't dry firmly enough, so method two simply wasn't possible. Necessity is the mother of invention, so I took a different approach which is now method one.

METHOD ONE

Use in humid conditions on a freshly iced and airbrushed cake.

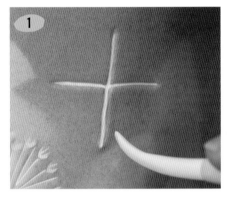  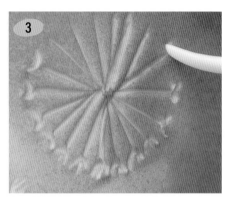

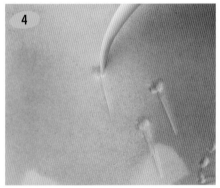 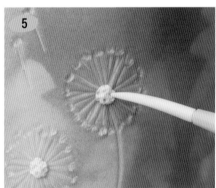 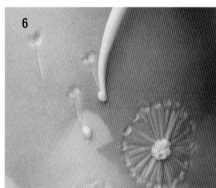

1. Take a veining tool and, pressing it into your soft icing, draw a cross.

2. Next, add more radial lines to form a circle.

3. Create parachutes by scraping away 'C' shapes on top of each radial line. Fill each 'C' with small lines until the seed head is complete.

4. Add a stem to each seed head, then a few individual parachutes as desired.

5. For the centres, press small balls of white paste in position. Add texture using the end of the tool.

6. Finally, add seeds to the individual parachutes.

METHOD TWO

Use in dry conditions on dry icing and dried airbrushing.

Working on a dried cake surface, take a craft knife and, with its blade slightly tilted, scrape away and create the seed heads as above. You will probably find that you will be able to make them more detailed using this method.

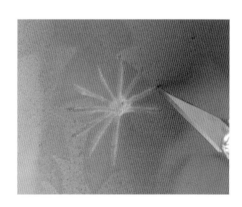

MAKING THE LARGE DANDELION SEED HEAD

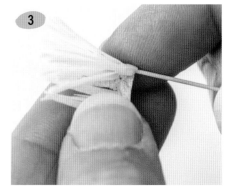

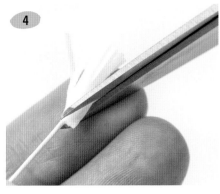

1. Cut white wafer paper into 2cm (¾in) wide strips. Holding approximately four strips in your hand at once, cut repeatedly into the strips with a sharp pair of scissors to a depth of 1.5cm (⁹⁄₁₆in). Next, cut the fringed strips into lengths of approximately 2.5cm (1in). You will need approximately sixty. Then, using wire cutters, cut the white floristry wires into 3.5cm (1⅜in) lengths.

2. Take a damp paintbrush and dampen the rough side of the uncut section of a fringed wafer paper piece as shown.

3. Wrap the wafer paper around one end of a cut wire. Squeeze the paper onto the wire with your fingers to make sure a firm bond is formed.

4. Using your scissors, shape by cutting away small triangles of wafer paper from either side of the wire as shown. Insert the wire vertically into the polystyrene block to dry.

5. To create the floating parachutes, cut longer lengths of wire then, using the parachute template (see page 137) to guide you, wrap a second strip of frilled wafer paper around the wire so that the tips of the parachute lie just below the seed, as shown.

Tip

Try to make your cuts as close as possible so that the parachutes will look nice and delicate.

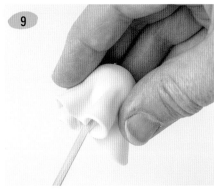

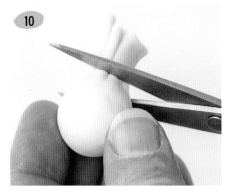

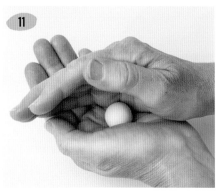

6. Once the parachutes are dry and firmly attached to their wires, open each parachute using very gentle steam. I used a pan of barely simmering water but you could use a steamer as long as you are careful: remember, steam can burn! Open up the parachutes by holding them one at a time above the steam. The steam will soften the paper and the chute will open up. Encourage it to do so by using your fingers.

7. To make the seeds, roll small balls of brown modelling paste. Next, place a parachute over the template. Then, using a brush, dampen the wire. Pick up a ball of brown modelling paste and wrap it around the dampened wire.

8. Squeeze both ends of the seed with your fingers to shape and firmly attach. Repeat.

9. Place the 2cm (¾in) polystyrene ball onto the barbecue skewer and cover with sugar glue. Roll out the cream modelling paste and drape over the ball as shown.

10. Squeeze the ends together, remove the skewer and cut away the excess paste with a pair of scissors.

11. Roll the covered ball in the palm of your hand to smooth and redistribute the paste more evenly. Once you are happy with the shape, place the ball back onto its skewer.

12. Trim the wires extending out of the seeds to 5mm (³⁄₁₆in). Then, using flat-nose pliers, carefully start inserting parachutes into the sides and top of the ball as shown.

13. Texture the front of the ball by pressing the small end of a ball tool repeatedly into the soft modelling paste.

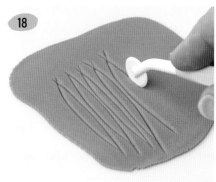

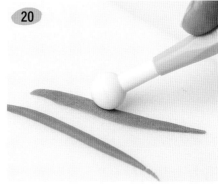

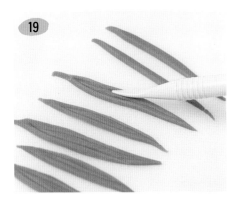

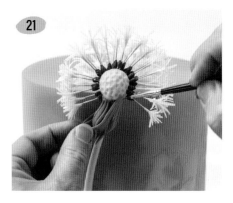

14. Continue to add parachutes until a quarter of the ball is completely covered. Insert a barbecue skewer or cocktail stick into the top edge of your cake at a 45-degree angle. Place your seed head onto this and secure with orange royal icing.

15. To make the stem, warm up some pale green modelling paste by kneading. Next, add some white vegetable fat to stop the paste getting sticky and then dip the paste in cooled boiled water to soften it. Place the softened paste into the barrel of the sugar shaper and the large round disc into the top and screw together. Pump the shaper until the pressure has built up and the paste is released from the extruder. Squeeze out a length that is long enough to create the stem.

Place on your work surface and thin one end by rolling the paste between your fingers. You are looking to make a tapered stem. Leave on your work surface to firm up a little.

16. To stick the stem in place, firstly paint a smooth curved line on the surface of your cake below the large seed head, using sugar glue. Cut the thinner end of the stem straight and attach under the seed head before placing the stem over your painted glue line.

17. Cut away the excess where the stem meets the board.

18. Cut green bracts freehand from thinly rolled-out flower paste using a cutting wheel. They should be about 5cm (2in) or so in length.

19. Place the bracts on a foam pad and add two veins to each bract with a dresden tool.

20. Soften all the edges using a ball tool.

21. Attach the bracts in place, using sugar glue, and position to give movement. Continue to add the prepared parachutes, leaving part of the textured centre uncovered.

WIRED LEAVES

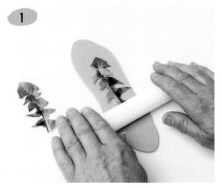

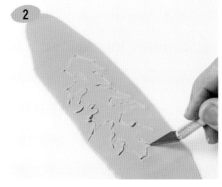

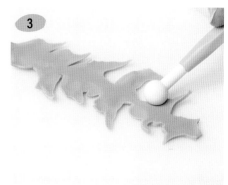

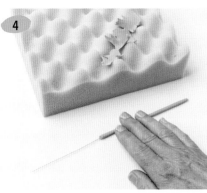

1. You will need two cut-out paper leaves approximately 8.5cm (3⅜in) and 11cm (4⅜in) long; resize as necessary. Roll out some green flower paste and place one of the paper templates on top. Roll over this with a small rolling pin.

2. Cut around the outline using a craft knife.

3. Place the leaf on the foam pad and run a ball tool over all the edges of the leaf to thin and frill slightly. Position on waffle foam to give more shape to the leaf and to allow the paste to firm up.

4. To give the leaf more stability, roll a sausage of green flower paste. Insert a dampened wire, then use your hand to even out and thin the paste further.

Note

There are a number of different ways of adding wires to leaves, so, by all means, use an alternative method if you wish to.

5. Attach the covered wire to the back of the leaf using sugar glue, then bend the wire to give more shape. Place the leaf back onto the waffle foam and create the second wired leaf.

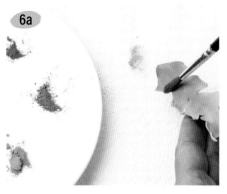

6a

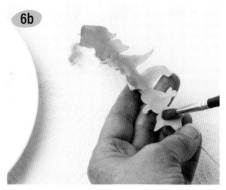

6b

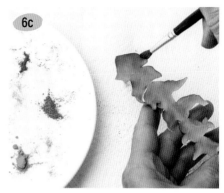

6c

7

8

9

6. Place a selection of greens and a deep blue dust on a plate. Begin dusting a leaf by adding a mid-green to the top (a), then moving down to a light green at the bottom (b), over-dusting to blend and change the colours. Add the blue dust to the edges of the leaf (c).

7. Once you have dusted both sides of both leaves, steam the dust using a steamer or the steam from a pan of simmering water to set the dusts.

8. Once dry, cut the excess wire away from the leaves and stick in position on the cake using orange royal icing.

9. Mix white edible dust with a little water and paint delicate veins onto both leaves using a fine paintbrush.

FINISHING TOUCHES

Bend the wires of the drifting parachutes as desired and insert into the centre of the polystyrene ball as shown. Add as many or as few as you wish.

Attach a suitable ribbon to the edge of your board using a non-toxic glue stick.

> ### Note
> Remember to tell the recipient of your cake about the non-edible items – i.e. the wires, cocktail stick and polystyrene ball. These should all be removed before cutting the cake.

BRENDA THE BRANDHILL SHEEP

Cute, cuddly sheep and gambolling lambs are the subject of many nursery rhymes, children's stories, animated films and ancient proverbs. So why not cake?

'Gambolling is happiness in motion.'
– Joan Jarvis Ellison (b. 1948), from the book
Shepherdess: Notes from the Field.

THE INSPIRATION

Until very recently, I had the great privilege of living on Brandhill in rural south Shropshire, UK. Living on top of a hill did have its drawbacks, especially when the winds blew, but it was an idyllic setting. A setting where, in the spring, I could watch sheep with their lambs on a daily basis, outside my back door. Brenda is one such sheep whom I chose to immortalize in cake form. The landscape either side of Brenda was my view – Titterstone Clee, Wenlock Edge and Brandhill Gutter. For me, this is a very special cake that will always remind me of my time on Brandhill. I'm rather taken with Brenda – I hope you are too.

1. *A mule ewe with her lamb;*
2. *The view from my back door, down Brandhill Gutter and across to Titterstone Clee Hill;*
3. *Panorama of the South Shropshire Hills: Brown Clee is on the left, Titterstone Clee on the right, with Wenlock Edge below.*

YOU WILL NEED

MATERIALS

- Cake – 18cm (7in) diameter × 15cm (6in) height – baked in two halves
- 1.2kg (2⅝lb) white sugarpaste (fondant)
- CMC/Tylose/gum – if using soft sugarpaste (fondant) or working in humid conditions
- Buttercream or chocolate ganache to add as a base coat before the sugarpaste (fondant)
- Modelling paste: 30g (1oz) white, 100g (3½oz) cream, 5g (⅛oz) yellow, 20g (¾oz) green
- Edible food dusts – a selection of colours including white
- Cocoa butter

- White vegetable fat
- Sugar glue (see page 17)
- Piece of dry spaghetti

EQUIPMENT AND TOOLS

- 23cm (9in) hardboard cake board
- 5mm- (³⁄₁₆in-) deep spacers
- Waxed paper/tracing paper
- Kitchen paper
- Template (see page 137)
- A4 – 297 x 210mm (11¾ x 8¼in) – plastic document wallet
- Pencil and eraser
- Glass-headed dressmakers' pins
- Cutting wheel

- Dresden tool
- Scriber
- Scissors
- Rolling pin
- Palette knife
- Ball tool
- Selection of paintbrushes
- White plates
- Source of heat – simmering pan of hot water or a tea-light in a pot warmer
- Sugar shaper (sugar extruder) and assorted discs
- Small daisy mould
- Length of 5mm (³⁄₁₆in) green ribbon
- Non-toxic glue stick

PREPARING THE CAKE

Level, stack and cover your baked cakes with white sugarpaste (fondant) to create one 15cm (6in) tall cake with sharp edges, following the instructions in the Techniques section (see pages 22–24).

Place centrally on the 23cm (9in) cake board. Roll out white sugarpaste (fondant) into a long strip between 5mm (³⁄₁₆in) spacers. Cut one edge straight, then wrap the paste around the cake to cover the board. Trim as necessary and place to one side to dry.

PAINTING THE SKY

1. Place some yellow, peach, orange, pink, lilac, light blue and white food dust individually around the sides of a white plate, then add a little cocoa butter to the centre. Position the plate over a source of heat. You can either use a simmering pan of water or a tea-light in a pot warmer or suitable container. Once the gentle heat has begun to melt the cocoa butter, mix a little into the white and yellow dusts to create a pale yellow paint.

2. Load a large, flat brush with the mixed paint and apply with horizontal sweeping strokes to the cake to create a band of colour at a height of approximately 10cm (4in). Keep the paint mix fairly dry to give a light, feathery finish to your strokes.

3. Mix the peach, orange and white dusts with cocoa butter and add a layer of paint above the yellow band.

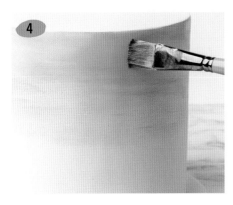

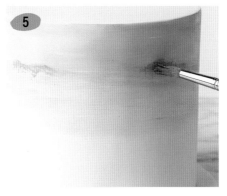

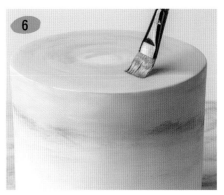

4. Next, add a light blue band on top of this.

5. Mix up some lilac paint, adding a touch of pink, and add a few clouds to the top of the orange layer as shown above. With a dry brush, blend these brush strokes to make the clouds appear wispy.

6. Paint the top of the cake to complete the sky.

CREATING THE HILLS

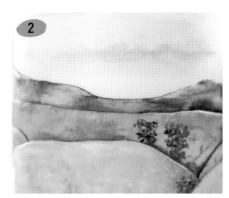

1. Measure the diameter of your cake. Then cut a piece of waxed or tracing paper the same length plus 1cm (⅜in) overlap × 15cm (6in) high. You can either use my design, based on the Shropshire hills as seen from Brandhill, as a reference, or if you are feeling creative have a go at creating your own landscape from either a photograph or your imagination. Either way, start by sketching the distant hills using a pencil. The maximum height of your hills should be around 10cm (4in).

2. Once you are happy with your horizon, start adding the layers of hills that create the finished scene (shown on the right from different angles). Draw the layers of hills onto the paper template as shown in step 1.

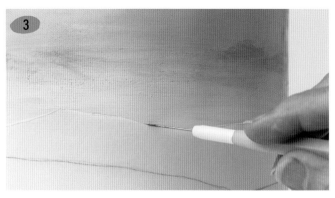

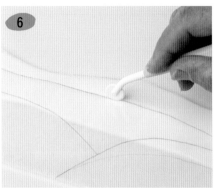

Tip

Remember that if you are using a soft sugarpaste (fondant) or working in humid conditions, you will probably need to add a little CMC/Tylose/gum to strengthen the paste to prevent it distorting too much when you lift it.

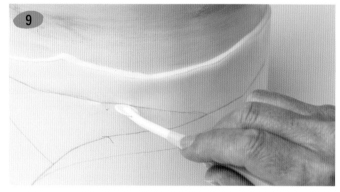

3. With scissors, cut along the horizon line of your tracing to remove the sky. Place the resulting hill template around the cake and secure it in place. Next, run a scriber along the edge of the template to scribe the shapes of the distant hills onto the cake.

4. Roll out white sugarpaste 2–3mm (¹⁄₁₆–¹⁄₈in) thick into a long thin strip large enough to fit around the cake.

5. Place the template over the rolled-out paste. Using a large cutting wheel, cut firmly along the outline of the distant hills , then remove the excess paste.

6. Roll your cutting wheel along the top of the hills below the horizon, pressing firmly. You are aiming to indent the paste under the template to create cutting lines, so check that you have pressed firmly enough before removing the template completely.

7. Next, smooth and round the top edge of the distant hills, using the heat of a finger.

8. Using the larger end of the cutting wheel, cut along each of the indented cutting lines. Remove the excess. Then thin the paste by running a small rolling pin over this cut edge, away from the prepared hills.

9. Using sugar glue and the scribed placement line, attach the hills in position on the cake. Align the template back on top of the cake and run your cutting wheel firmly over the soft paste of the lower hill line as shown above.

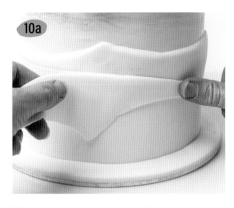

10a

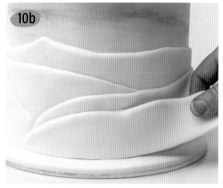

10b

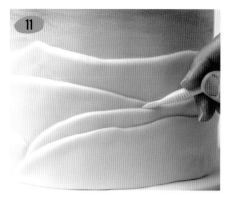

11

10. Using the same process, make and attach the remaining hills, working from the back to the front of the scene.

11. Once you are happy with your landscape, take a dresden tool and neaten up any joins as necessary.

PAINTING THE HILLS

Not all brands of edible dusts are created equal and some work better than others for cocoa painting. You are looking to create an opaque paint so you may find that you need to add some edible white dust into colours to create this.

Remember, if you haven't painted with cocoa butter before, you can experiment first on a spare piece of sugarpaste (fondant) until you are happy with the results.

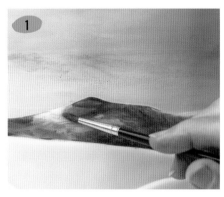

1

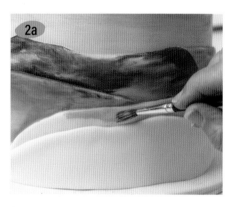

2a

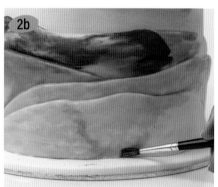

2b

1. I recommend that you start around the back of the cake so by the time you reach the front you are feeling confident. Choose or mix shades of purple and blue dusts. Place these shades on the edge of a white plate and add some cocoa butter. Position the plate over a source of heat and once the cocoa butter has melted, mix a little into the dust colours to create a thick paint. Dip your paintbrush into the paint and apply to the distant hills in small sweeping strokes. Use a dry brush to help blend one colour into another.

2. Mix up a variety of green paints and paint over the lower hills as desired, changing from a blue-green in the distance to a lime green in the foreground and on the board.

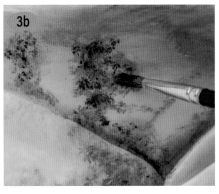

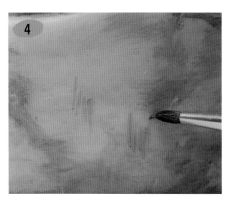

3. Once you are happy with your landscape, start adding hedges and trees by using small dabs of the darker greens.

4. Finish off by adding vertical grass stems in the foreground.

CREATING THE BODIES

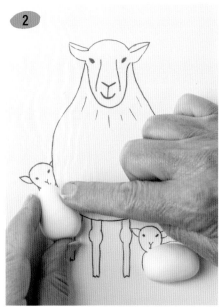

1. Trace the sheep template (see page 137) onto tracing paper or waxed paper. Decide where your sheep will stand on your painted cake – mine are standing to the right of Brandhill Gutter! Secure the template in place with dressmakers' pins. Press firmly with a scriber and work around the body outlines of the sheep and her lambs. Remove the template and ensure that the scribed lines are visible – they are to aid placement.

2. Place a copy of the sheep template into a plastic document wallet. Using 10g (⅜oz) of sugarpaste per lamb, roll and shape each ball of the paste to fit the template.

3. For the sheep, roll 90g (3⅛oz) of sugarpaste in a ball and then an oval. Place this oval onto the template and squash and shape using the palm of your hand until it fits the sides of the template but is slightly short of the top of the head. Smooth paste away from the head area to fatten her chest.

4. Using the scribed lines for guidance, attach the three bodies in place on the painted cake using sugar glue.

5. To make the legs, roll sausages of paste to fit the template. Thin either side of the knees using a dresden tool and a small rolling action. Indent each end vertically, using the sharp end of a dresden tool, to create the two digits for each hoof.

6. Attach the legs in place using sugar glue and adjust using a dresden tool as necessary. Then paint sugar glue over the bodies of the sheep and her lambs.

7. To make the lambs' wool, soften some of the white modelling paste by adding a little white vegetable fat and cooled boiled water. Knead until it is really quite soft. Place inside the sugar shaper together with the smallest mesh disc. Push down the plunger and pump using the handle to squeeze out short lengths of paste. If the paste doesn't come out easily, it isn't soft enough, so add more white fat and water.

8. Remove these tufts of paste with a dresden tool and attach to the pre-glued lambs' bodies. Place the wool so it hangs down and adjust positioning with a dresden tool.

9. To make the sheep's wool, which is scruffier, soften the cream modelling paste and place in the sugar shaper with the large mesh disc. Squeeze out 1.5cm (⁹⁄₁₆in) lengths, remove a few with a dresden tool, then pinch their ends together.

10. Starting at the base of the sheep, stick these clumps of wool in place. Next, using a finger and dresden tool, pull down some of the wool strands to elongate them.

11. Continue to add the sugar wool, stretching it slightly until all but the neck of the sheep is covered.

CREATING THE LAMBS' HEADS

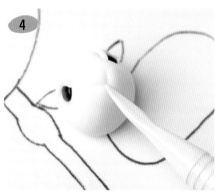

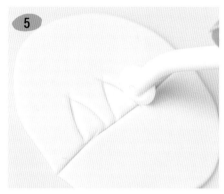

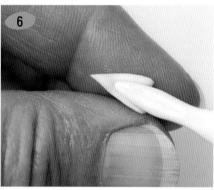

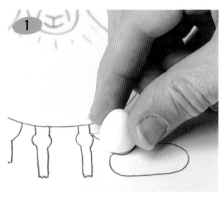

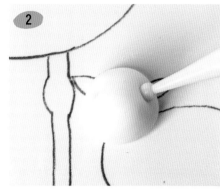

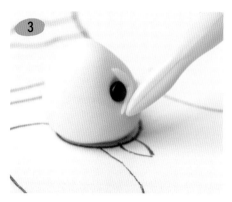

1. Roll a small ball of white paste into a cone to fit the first lamb's head on the template.

2. Indent eye sockets on either side of the head using a small ball tool.

3. Fill each eye socket with a small ball of black modelling paste. Then roll two small tapered sausages of white paste and attach one above each eye, in a smooth curve. Adjust as necessary.

4. Mark a 'Y' shape using a dresden tool to create the lamb's nose.

5. Roll out some white modelling paste and cut out two ears, freehand, using a cutting wheel.

6. Shape the ears by pressing a dresden tool into the soft paste.

7. Attach both the head and ears in place using sugar glue. Repeat for the second lamb.

CREATING THE SHEEP'S HEAD

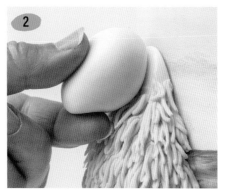

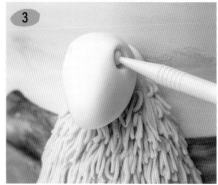

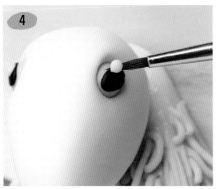

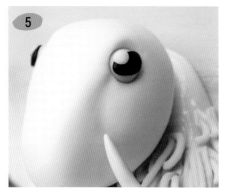

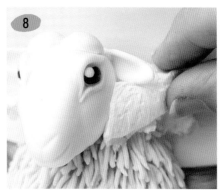

1. Insert a short length of dry spaghetti into the neck of the sheep to help support the head.

2. Roll 16g (⅝oz) of white paste into a ball, then a cone and position onto the cake, using sugar glue. Gently pinch the cone on the sides and top to bottom as shown.

3. Create eye sockets, using the small end of a ball tool. Enlarge the socket slightly by pushing upwards to help square off the sheep's forehead.

4. Fill each eye socket with a ball of green paste, then add small black rectangles of paste for the pupils and white dots for light spots.

5. Shape and define the cheeks by pressing a dresden tool into the paste below the eyes as shown.

6. Using the sharp end of the dresden tool, indent a 'Y' for the nose and a smiling mouth.

7. Roll four small tapered sausages of white paste and attach these above and below each eye. Shape using a dresden tool.

8. Add two small flattened balls of white paste to the top of the sheep's head. Then create ears as you did for the lambs (see opposite). Stick these in place, using scrunched-up pieces of kitchen paper for support while the glue dries.

9. Let down a little white sugarpaste by mixing it with water until it is of a thick paint consistency. Paint this over the top of the sheep's head to disguise any joins in the paste and to add texture.

10. Once the ears are secure, remove the kitchen paper and cover the sheep's neck with sugar wool.

PAINTING THE SHEEP AND LAMBS

1. Using a mixture of browns, creams, white and black dusts mixed into melted cocoa butter, paint markings onto the faces of the sheep. Note, no two sheep are identical.

2. Paint over the sheep's wool to highlight and add interest.

FINISHING TOUCHES

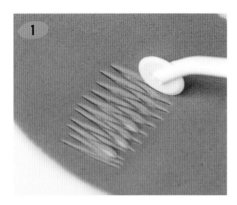

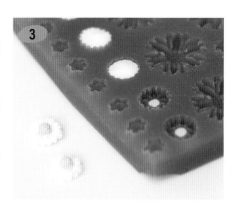

1. Roll out some thin green modelling paste. Roll a cutting wheel backwards and forwards to create thin triangles of paste as shown.

2. Pick up these triangles in small clumps and attach them around the base of the cake.

3. To create small daisies, place balls of yellow modelling paste in the central cavities of a daisy mould. Place balls of white modelling paste on top. Press down firmly. Remove any excess paste, then flex the mould to release the daisies.

4. Attach the daisies to the cake using sugar glue. Finally, add a green ribbon to the edge of the cake drum using a non-toxic glue stick.

'SARAH'S MIRACLE': BABY SHOWER

Baby showers are a delightful celebration for a soon-to-be mother – a time before the baby arrives when a new mum-to-be can enjoy being with her female friends and family; it's a time when small gifts are given for the baby.
In the UK, baby showers are a relatively new tradition but I think they're a wonderful way to celebrate the last month of pregnancy. I wish they'd been around when I was expecting!

THE INSPIRATION

After hearing how much everyone enjoyed my daughter's friend's baby shower, I knew I wanted to include a baby shower cake in this book. While wondering what exactly to create, I remembered Sarah Pickles and her story. Sarah is an amazing woman who I met through business networking. The first time we met, she was heavily pregnant and had an incredible story to tell. I learned that Sarah is a breast cancer survivor from a family with a history of the disease. She had been told by her doctors that she wouldn't be able to have any more children, even by IVF. She has written a book to help others about her experiences, called *The Shock Factor*, which, if I remember rightly, was why she was attending the networking event.

However, Sarah's story has an incredibly heart-warming ending. Two years after her diagnosis and starting IVF, Sarah experienced back pains. Thinking the disease had returned, she was rushed to hospital for a scan. There was a shadow near her spine, but amazingly, this turned out to be a miracle baby – Sarah was actually pregnant!

Thank you, Sarah, for being my inspiration.

Tip

You could turn your cake into a gender reveal cake by adding colour to the cake mix itself.

YOU WILL NEED

MATERIALS

- Cake – 15cm (6in) diameter × 18cm (7in) height
- 1.1kg (2⅜in) white sugarpaste (fondant)
- Buttercream or chocolate ganache to add as a base coat before the sugarpaste (fondant)
- Airbrush colours: peach, pink
- Modelling paste for flowers: pink, orange, pale orange, cream
- Edible food dusts: a selection of colours to colour the modelling chocolate (see below)
- Modelling chocolate coloured with food dusts as follows: 180g (6⅜oz) flesh, 70g (2½oz) dark brown, 15g (½oz) turquoise, 5g (⅛oz) lime green, 35g (1¼oz) light blue, 5g (⅛oz) white, 5g (⅛oz) pink

- White vegetable fat
- Sugar glue (see page 17)
- Pink food dust
- Pink royal icing: a small amount to attach flowers

EQUIPMENT AND TOOLS

- 20cm (8in) cake board
- Template × 2 (see page 138)
- Two A4 – 297 x 210mm (11¾ x 8¼in) – plastic document wallets
- Airbrush
- Craft knife
- Self-healing cutting mat
- Thin permanent marker pen
- Plastic lid or milk bottle to make masks
- Wooden barbecue skewers
- PVA glue
- Daisy centre mould or stamp

- Silicone modelling tools: one pointed, one flat-ended
- Smoother
- Blossom cutters of different sizes
- Foam pad
- Waffle foam and polystyrene flower formers (or similar)
- Glass-headed dressmakers' pins
- Cutting wheel
- Dresden tool
- Scissors
- Rolling pin
- Ball tool
- Selection of paintbrushes
- Sugar shaper (sugar extruder) and assorted discs
- Narrow ribbon to cover the edge of the board
- Non-toxic glue stick

PREPARING AND AIRBRUSHING THE CAKE

> **Note**
> I used milk modelling chocolate as a base for the dark brown hair colour and white modelling chocolate for all the other colours.

Level, stack and cover your baked cakes with white sugarpaste (fondant) to create one 18cm (7in) tall cake with sharp edges, following the instructions in the Techniques section (see pages 22–24).

Place your covered cake centrally on the 20cm (8in) cake board. Roll out the remaining white sugarpaste (fondant) into a long strip, long enough to fit around your cake board. Cut one edge straight. With the cut edge abutting your decorated cake, position the paste strip on the cake board. Cut to fit and blend the join with the heat of your hand. Cut away the excess from the edge of the board using a palette knife.

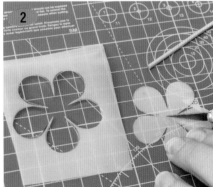

1. To make flower masks for the airbrushing, you will need: three blossom cutters of different shapes and sizes, some flat firm but thin plastic such as a margarine lid or milk bottle; a permanent marker pen, a self-healing cutting mat and a craft knife.

2. Place a blossom cutter onto the plastic and draw around its outline, using the marker pen. Take your craft knife and carefully cut out the blossom shape. Next, cut a small cross in the centre of the blossom. Insert the end of a wooden barbecue skewer into the cross to act as a handle. Stick in place using PVA glue and allow to dry. Repeat using the other two cutters so you have three masks that are all different.

3. Fill your airbrush inkwell with peach airbrush colour (see page 27). Hold one of the masks as close as you can to the cake without touching its surface. Hold the nozzle of your airbrush 30cm (12in) or so away from your cake and gently apply the colour around the edges of the mask. Repeat until you have gone all the way around the cake.

4. Next, fill the inkwell with some pink airbrush colour. Using the masks and airbrush as before, spray pink colour but this time overlapping the blossoms with the blossoms of the first peach layer.

5. Decorate the top of the cake in the same fashion, again starting with the peach before changing to the pink.

6. Continue adding layers of colour until you are happy with the effect. Leave to dry.

THE FLOWERS

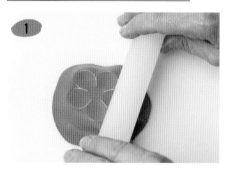

1. Roll out some of the pink modelling paste quite thinly. Place it over one of your blossom cutters and roll over the cutting edges with a rolling pin. Rub over the cutter with your thumb to remove any feathering.

2. Turn the cutter over and use a paintbrush to help remove the flower from the cutter if necessary. Press a ball of contrasting-coloured modelling paste into a daisy centre mould. Remove from the mould and stick in the centre of the flower using sugar glue.

3. Place to dry either in the dips of waffle foam or in a flower former of the correct size for your cutter. Repeat to make blossoms of different sizes. You will need approximately four large, eight medium and ten small. Create an additional medium-sized flower from pink modelling chocolate for the hair decoration (on page 84).

THE FIGURE

Tip

If the modelling chocolate is very hard, warm it in a microwave for a few seconds before kneading

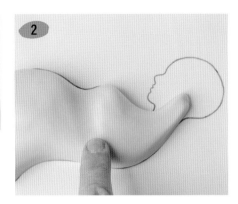

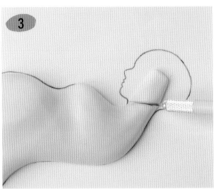

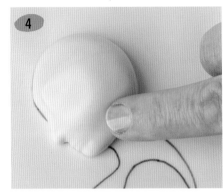

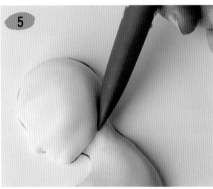

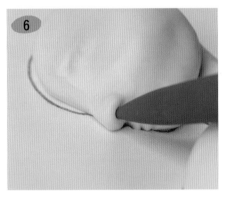

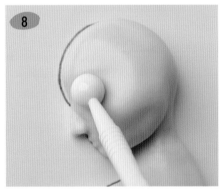

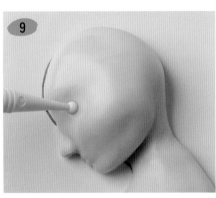

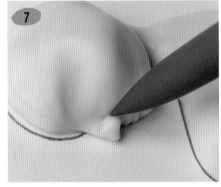

1. Place your figure templates in plastic document wallets. Warm up 130g (4½oz) of flesh-coloured modelling chocolate. Place the warmed chocolate onto the body of the template and stroke it into shape. Define the bulge of her belly and round off her back.

2. Use the warmth of your fingers to extend and stroke her neck into shape, then indent and shape the area below her bustline.

3. Using a craft knife, cut away the excess paste at the neck.

4. Warm and roll 30g (1oz) of flesh modelling chocolate into a ball for the head. Place on top of your second template and begin to shape the ball to fit the template outline. Flatten the eye area with a finger, pinch out the nose and the chin,

using the heat of your fingers to soften and mould the chocolate. You are just aiming for a rough approximation at this stage.

5. Pick up the head and place it on the body. Blend the neck into the head using a pointed silicone modelling tool.

6. Insert the pointed silicone modelling tool into the nostril to enlarge and shape.

7. Next, shape the outside using the same tool, indenting it into the soft paste as shown.

8. For the eye, indent a large ball tool into the eye socket area.

9. Using a small ball tool, indent the centre of the eye socket.

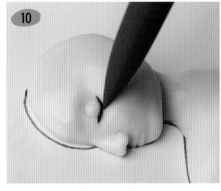

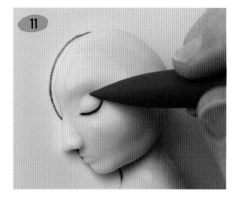

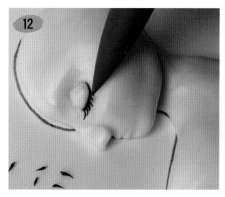

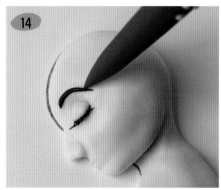

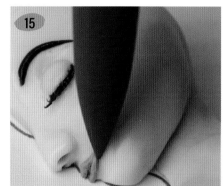

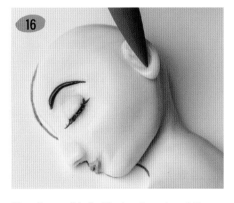

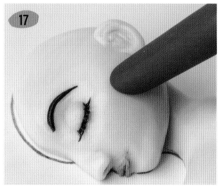

10. Roll a small ball of flesh-coloured modelling chocolate to fit the indented hole snugly. Next, roll a very thin sausage of black modelling chocolate and place in the position to make the base of the eyelashes, as shown. Use a silicone modelling tool to aid placement.

11. Using the same tool, blend the top of the eyelid into the face.

12. Roll some tiny tapered sausages of black modelling chocolate to create individual eyelashes. Pick these up using the modelling tool and attach them to the black eyelash base, as shown.

13. Continue until the row of eyelashes is complete.

14. Roll a tapered black sausage for the eyebrow, position, trim and shape as desired.

15. For the lips, roll two small tapered sausages of pink modelling chocolate. Place in position on the mouth. Using your modelling tool, blend the pink into the flesh along the natural lip line. Create the Cupid's bow of the top lip and shape the body of the lip into the lip corner. Adjust the angle of the mouth to give a pleasing expression.

16. For the ear, roll a small ball of flesh-coloured modelling chocolate and position it on the side of the head, above the jawline. Flatten the ball slightly with a finger. The ear should lie in line with the bottom of the nose and top of the eyebrow. Using your tool, blend the front side of the ear into the flesh of the face, then create the ear lobe and helix. Note that the ear doesn't need to be detailed as it will be covered by the hair.

17. Finally for this stage, define the cheekbones using a flat-ended silicone modelling tool.

DRESSING THE FIGURE

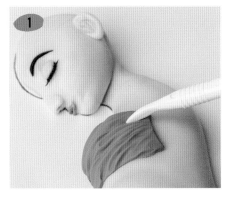

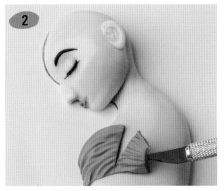

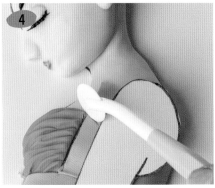

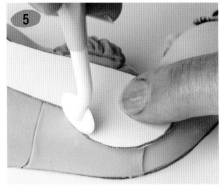

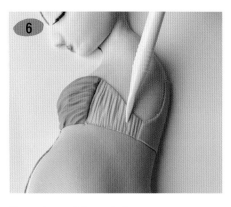

1. Roll out some of the turquoise modelling chocolate into a 2cm- (¾in-) wide strip and drape it over the bust area of your figure. Use a craft knife to cut the paste to shape on the bust. Add ruching to the fabric by running the side of a dresden tool through the soft paste in short strokes.

2. Use your craft knife to cut away the excess paste on the bust as shown.

3. Thinly roll out the light blue modelling chocolate. Place over the figure using one edge to form the dress's waist seam. Smooth the paste over the body with the heat of your hand, then using a cutting wheel, carefully cut away the excess modelling chocolate.

4. Roll out a 2.5cm- (1in-) wide strip of light blue modelling chocolate. Cut one edge straight and then another at right angles. Position on the body above the waist seam to the side of the bust; this section creates the side and back of the dress. Cut the back to size using a cutting wheel. Next cut out the arm template and place onto the body. Using the template to guide you, cut away the excess paste from the front of the dress...

5. ...and around the armhole.

6. Add texture to this section by using the narrow end of your dresden tool to make vertical strokes. Roll thin sausages of lime green paste and attach these on top of the seam of the dress, under the bust and around the armhole.

ADDING THE ARM AND COMPLETING THE DRESS

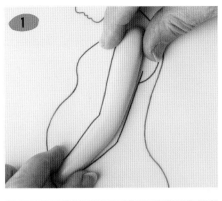

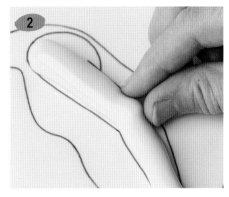

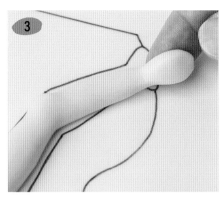

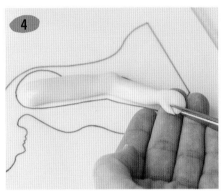

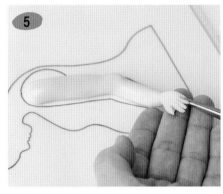

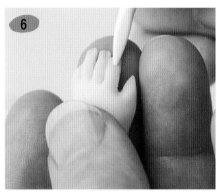

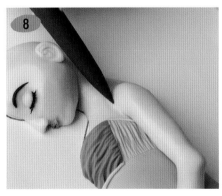

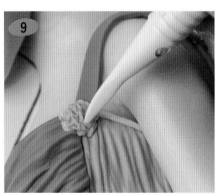

1. Using the template as a guide, roll a tapered sausage of flesh-coloured modelling chocolate.

2. Create the elbow by firstly pinching the modelling chocolate as shown and then again at 90 degrees to the first.

3. Thin the wrist by rolling it between your fingers, then pinch the hand flat.

4. Using scissors, remove a small triangle to form a thumb.

5. Make three cuts to create four fingers.

6. Press the end of your dresden tool into the end of each finger to create nails. Then use a ball tool to cup the hand slightly.

7. Position the arm on the shoulder and blend the paste into the body with the heat of your fingers.

8. Use a silicone modelling tool to adjust as necessary. Position the arm so that it looks natural; remember, bones don't bend. If your arm is still very soft, you might find it easier to let it firm up a little before adding it to the body.

9. Cut a thin shoulder strap from rolled-out turquoise modelling chocolate and position it over the top of the arm. Cut to size with a craft knife. Add a small fabric flower to disguise the join at the front. Do this by rolling small balls of lime green and blue paste, placing the blue ball on top of the green and then texturing both with the sharp end of a dresden tool.

10. Finally, add a few stitches by indenting a pointed tool into the end of the strap at the back.

PLACING THE FIGURE ON THE CAKE

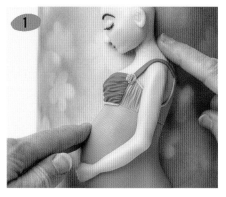

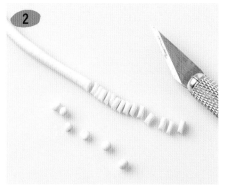

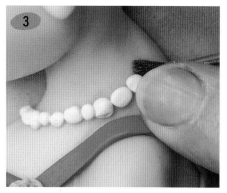

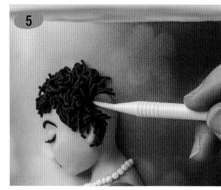

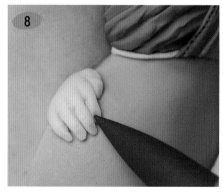

1. Decide which is the front of your cake, then carefully pick up the figure and position her there. Smooth the paste at the joins where she meets the cake, using your fingers to remove any gaps.

2. To make the pearls for the necklace, roll a thin sausage of white modelling chocolate. Slice the sausage into sections of the same size, then roll each of these sections into a ball.

3. Warm the neck area of the figure using the heat of your finger, then attach the white balls to form a necklace, using your finger and a dry paintbrush.

4. Warm up the dark brown modelling chocolate. Roll it into a sausage and place it inside a sugar shaper together with the large mesh disc. Push out the air, then squeeze out short lengths. Remove these short lengths with a dresden tool, wipe the disc clean and squeeze until you have a selection of tufts.

5. Warm the head of your figure using your fingers, then attach the tufts of hair to create a hairstyle, adding movement as you go, using a dresden tool.

6. Press the large end of a ball tool into the hair above the ear. Add the flower made earlier into this recess.

7. Dip a brush into pink food dust, knock off the excess and then carefully apply to the cheeks as blusher.

8. Model a second hand from flesh-coloured modelling chocolate, shape as before, then cut across the palm at an angle and attach the hand to the top of the belly. Adjust the positioning of the fingers using a silicone modelling tool.

FINISHING TOUCHES

Attach a suitable, narrow ribbon to the edge of your board using a non-toxic glue stick.

Finally, carefully attach the modelling paste flowers made earlier (see page 79) using pink royal icing to secure them in place.

50 AND FABULOUS

Celebrations are part of all our lives and always have been.
We celebrate the passing of important milestones, we acknowledge the
progress we've made and mark the passage of time.
In an unpredictable world, celebrations provide structure and predictability,
a short interlude when time stands still; a time in which we celebrate our
achievements and appreciate what has gone before.
I believe that for all these occasions – and I hope you agree –
a celebration cake is a must!

INSPIRATION

Sugar quilling as a technique was on my list even before I started working on the
designs for this book; it appears in one of my previous books, and has proved to be
popular with my students. However, I wanted to explore its potential further, and
design a suitable full-sized cake.

The idea for this '50' cake was given to me by my commissioning editor, who
happened to mention that in 2020, the year in which this book was first published,
my publishers, Search Press, would be celebrating fifty years. To personalize the cake
for them, I've included a book, some balloons, champagne flutes – plus the sun and
mountains, which represent new horizons. This design is easy to adapt for your own
celebration – let me show you how.

*Three inspirational paper quilling
designs; flower motifs (1 and 3)
and colourful moth (2).*

YOU WILL NEED

MATERIALS

- Cake – 18cm (7in) diameter × 15cm (6in) height
- 1.2kg (2⅝lb) white sugarpaste (fondant)
- Buttercream or chocolate ganache to add as a base coat before the sugarpaste (fondant)
- Modelling paste: white and a selection of colours for the quilling
- White vegetable fat
- Sugar glue (see page 17)

EQUIPMENT AND TOOLS

- 25cm (10in) cake board
- '50' template (see page 139) – you could also create your own template using a computer
- Cutters:
  - 3.5cm (1⅜in) circle (by Lindy's Cakes)
  - Small teardrop (by Lindy's Cakes)
- Waxed paper/tracing paper
- Pencil and eraser
- Paper and coloured pencils
- Glass-headed dressmakers' pins
- Masking tape
- Scriber
- Craft knife
- Cocktail stick
- 1mm- (¹⁄₁₆in-) deep spacers
- Ruler
- Scissors
- Self-healing cutting mat
- Selection of paintbrushes
- Rolling pin
- Palette knife
- Ribbon
- Non-toxic glue stick

COVERING THE CAKE

Level, stack and cover your baked cakes with white sugarpaste to create one 15cm (6in) tall cake with sharp edges, following the instructions in the Techniques section (see pages 22–24).

Place your covered cake centrally on the 25cm (10in) cake drum. Roll out the remaining white sugarpaste into a strip long enough to fit around your cake board. Cut one straight edge. With the cut edge abutting your decorated cake, position the paste strip on the cake board. Cut to fit and blend the join with the heat of your hand. Cut away the excess from the edge of the board using a palette knife.

ADDING THE '50'

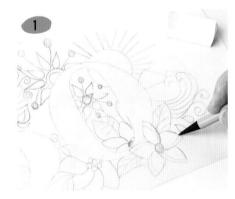

1. Cut your tracing paper into a strip the same height as your cake. Trace the '50' template or your own number onto the centre of your paper using a pencil. Now is your chance to really personalize your cake by drawing design elements relevant to the recipient of the cake. You can of course copy my design in its entirety or use sections of the design. Keep the details simple at this stage to avoid overcomplicating your design. You can leave your number complete, or cut into it as I have done with a flower.

2. Photocopy your finished design. Next, using colouring pencils, colour in your design, paying particular attention to the colours of your lines – the parts that will make up the quilling. Colouring your design should help you decide on the colours that you'll use. If you don't like the combinations you've chosen at this stage, simply make another copy of your original design and start again.

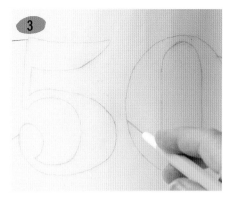

3

4

Tip

You might find it easier to pierce small holes through the number outline rather than scribe around it.

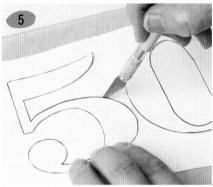

5

6

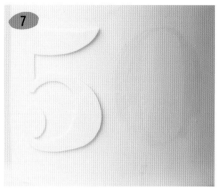

7

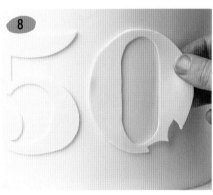

8

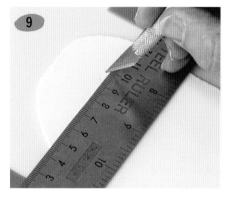

9

10

3. Cut a piece of waxed paper into a strip the same height as your cake. Trace the '50' template or your own number onto the centre of your paper using a pencil. Place the paper onto the front of your cake, securing in place with glass-headed dressmakers' pins. Take a scriber and scribe around all edges of the number.

4. Make a paper copy of your number template and cut it out using scissors. Use your traced design to remove any sections where your design cuts into the number.

5. Tape a piece of waxed paper to a small work board. Using the 1mm (¹⁄₁₆in) spacers, roll out some white modelling paste large enough to create your number. Place the paste on top of the board and leave for a few moments to firm up a fraction. Next, place your cut-out paper numbers on top of your modelling paste and carefully out around all the edges using a craft knife.

6. Remove all the excess paste to reveal your number.

7. Using the scribed lines on the cake, carefully infill the numbers with sugar glue using a paintbrush.

8. Once the modelling paste numbers are dry enough to be removed from the waxed paper and lifted without becoming distorted, attach them in place on the cake.

9. To make the border around the numbers, roll out a strip of white modelling paste between the 1mm (¹⁄₁₆in) spacers so that all the paste is of uniform thickness. Then, using a ruler and craft knife, indent marks at 5mm (³⁄₁₆in) intervals as shown.

10. Using these indents, cut out 5mm- (³⁄₁₆in-) wide strips and leave them on your work surface to firm up slightly.

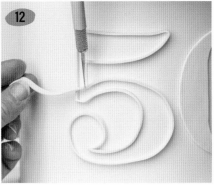

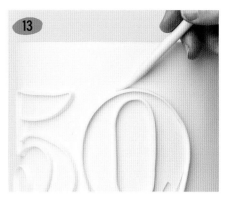

11. Meanwhile, paint sugar glue around the edge of the paste numbers on the cake.

12. Once the 5mm- (³⁄₁₆in-) wide strips are firm enough to be handled without stretching, pick them up and attach on their edges, to the outsides of the numbers. Take care with the placement of your joins and cut to size with a craft knife.

13. When attaching the strips, use the back of a dresden tool to press the lengths firmly up against the paste numbers as shown.

ADDING THE QUILLED DECORATIONS

How you approach your design will depend on the motifs you have included. I recommend that you study my following examples carefully, which describe the basic principles, and adapt these accordingly.

> ### Note
> The sides of the flower that rest inside the '0' of '50' are not completely covered, as the '0' itself provides the missing section.

PINK FLOWERS

1. Place a paper copy of the design onto a self-healing cutting mat. Using a craft knife cut out the whole and partial pink flower that lie at the bottom right of the '0'. Using the 1mm (¹⁄₁₆in) spacers, roll out some dark pink modelling paste. Place the cut-out flowers on top. Carefully cut around each paper flower using a craft knife as shown.

2. Next, cut from the centre along the edge of each petal. Remove the paper petals, then cut another line approximately 1.5mm (¹⁄₁₆in) away from the first cut that divides each petal from the next and remove this thin strip. Doing this allows the edges of the petals to be easily inserted without enlarging the flower.

3. Cut out 5mm- (¼in-) wide strips from dark pink, pink and white modelling paste that has been rolled out between 1mm (¹⁄₁₆in) spacers. Without moving your cut-out petals, paint all their cut edges with sugar glue using a fine paintbrush. Next, wrap a length of pink paste, on its edge, from the centre of a petal around the outside until it meets the next petal, using a dresden tool to press the strip gently onto the glue as you go. Cut away the excess paste and repeat until all the petals are complete.

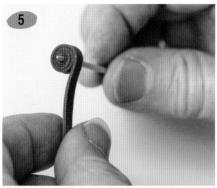

4. Paint the inside of each petal with sugar glue. Add one dark pink length of paste to each petal, as shown, cutting it to length in the centre of the flower. Follow this with a loose white scroll, again cutting to size in the centre. Allow the glue to firm up and the elements, stick together before lifting them with a palette knife and placing them in position on the cake, using sugar glue to secure.

5. To make the flower centres, pick up one end of a dark pink strip and gently press onto the tip of a cocktail stick. Roll the cocktail stick until you have six rounds of paste around the stick. Carefully slip the paste coil from the stick and cut away the excess paste. Secure the cut end of the strip to the coil using a damp paintbrush. Position in the centre of the full flower on the cake. For the half flower. Make another coil and cut to fit before glueing in place.

LEAVES

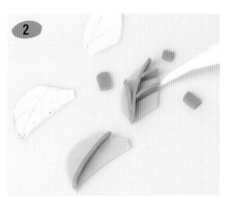

1. On a self-healing mat, cut out paper templates for the leaves that 'sit' on either side of the whole pink flower. Check their fit on the cake by placing the paper version in situ. You may need to make adjustments to your paper shapes so that they fit snugly. As you become more practised at this technique, you'll find you'll be able to judge spacing more easily and will not have to make as many adjustments.

2. Cut out the leaves from thinly rolled lime green modelling paste. Add veins using 4mm- (³⁄₁₆in-) wide strips, so that the leaf veins will lie at the same height as the outer leaf edges. Cut the veins to size as you go and press them together using a dresden tool as before.

3. Wrap 5mm- (³⁄₁₆in-) wide strips of lime green modelling paste around the edge of each leaf (the parts that don't abut the flower). Cut the tip of the leaves to a point using a craft knife.

4. Once the glue has dried enough to allow handling, pick up the leaves and attach in place on the cake.

THE MOUNTAINS AND THE SEA

Most elements are made off the cake and attached once complete; however, some – like the sea – are created in part and then assembled on the cake. Using cutters for some of the elements will also save you some time.

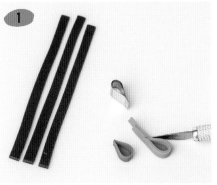

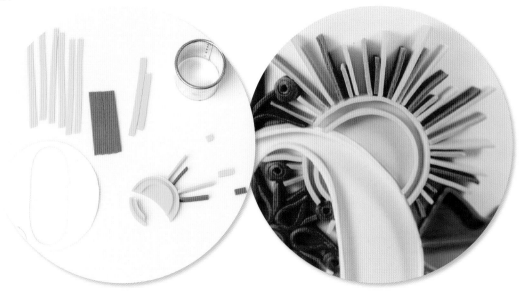

1. To make the water splashes, cut out small teardrops using the small teardrop cutter. Wrap each in a contrasting strip of blue and cut to size, as shown.

2. To make the open coils that represent the waves, make small tight coils using a cocktail stick as for the flower centre (see page 91), but this time, unravel them and place on your design template to harden enough to hold their shape.

3. Add to the cake to build up the design, cutting to size as required.

4. Add as many waves as you like, to complete.

ADDITIONAL ELEMENTS

These are laid-out examples of other elements of the design:

Sun

Champagne and balloons

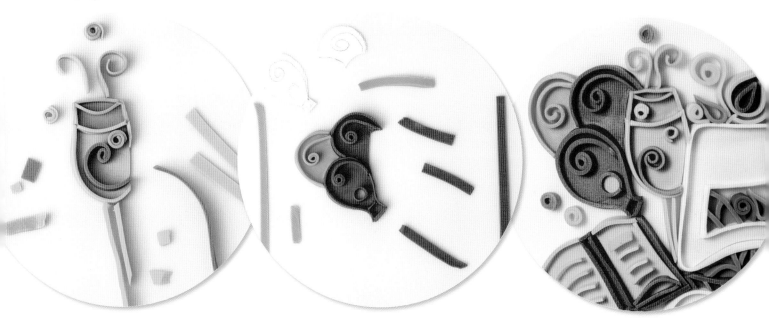

Scrolled flowers

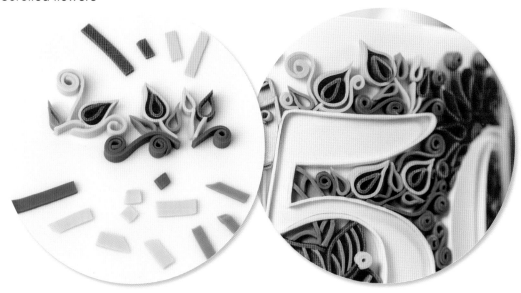

The principle is always the same:
- Cut out a shape to work on from your paper template;
- Remove 1.5mm- (¹⁄₁₆in-) wide sections from between the sugar versions of your shapes to allow for the quilling strips to be attached;
- Stick the sugar quilling strips, on their edges, to the shapes using sugar glue;
- Use 5mm- (³⁄₁₆in-) wide stripes around the edges of a shape;
- Use 4mm- (³⁄₁₆in-) wide stripes inside a shape.

FINISHING TOUCHES

Once you are happy with your design, add a ribbon to your cake board and secure it in place with a non-toxic glue stick.

KLIMT'S CAT

Cats are very special animals to many of us and as the
French novelist Colette (1873–1954) put it, 'Time spent
with a cat is never wasted.' Quite a few of my very early
cake-decorating books contain cat cakes, so the challenge
for me here was to take a completely different approach.

THE INSPIRATION

I've always been drawn to the work of the Austrian symbolist painter Gustav Klimt
(1862–1918) – his golden phase paintings are so vibrant, fascinating and detailed.
I love how Klimt blends reality with geometric patterns and fluid shapes.
I choose a black cat as the focal point of this cake design to give contrast to the
gold backdrop, inspired by Klimt. By doing so it made me think of my good friend
and fellow sugarcrafter Alan Dunn, who, as some of you may know, owns a black
cat called Bertie. I have since discovered other friends with black cats, too!

My friends' black cats have proven an inspiration:
1. Moriarty, Heather Nobel's cat;
2. Mips, Jill Ming's cat;
3. Moriarty.

YOU WILL NEED

MATERIALS

- Cake – 15cm (6in) diameter × 15cm (6in) height – baked in two halves
- 1kg (2¼lb) gold-coloured sugarpaste (fondant)
- Buttercream or chocolate ganache to add as a base coat before the sugarpaste (fondant)
- Modelling paste: 150g (5¼oz) black, plus 50–100g (1¾–3½oz) each of gold, red, pale pink, fuchsia pink, burgundy, peach, grey, light blue, blue, navy blue
- Edible metallic gold and bronze lustre dusts
- White vegetable fat
- Sugar glue (see page 17)
- Confectioners' glaze

EQUIPMENT AND TOOLS

- 23cm (9in) Stand It designer cake board
- Cat template (see page 140)
- Waxed paper/tracing paper
- Pencil and eraser
- Glass-headed dressmakers' pins
- White plate or paint palette
- Dresden tool
- Smoother
- Scriber
- Craft knife
- Sharp knife
- 5mm- (¼in-) deep spacers
- 1mm- (1⁄16in-) deep spacers
- Scissors
- Sugarcraft cutters:
  - Small oval and small equilateral triangle sets (by Lindy's Cakes)
- Rolling pin
- Palette knife
- No.s 4, 16, 17 and 18 piping tubes (by PME)
- Selection of paintbrushes
- Sugar shaper (sugar extruder) and assorted discs
- Plastic food wrap

PREPARING THE CAKE

Level, stack and cover your baked cakes with white sugarpaste to create one 15cm (6in) tall cake with sharp edges, following the instructions in the Techniques section (see pages 22–24). Allow the icing to dry.

CREATING THE BACKDROP

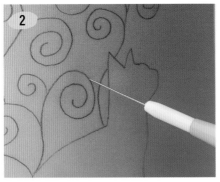
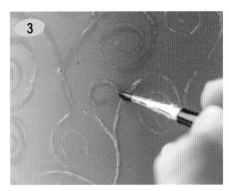

1. Measure the diameter of your cake. Cut a piece of waxed or tracing paper the same length plus 1cm (⅜in) overlap × 15cm (6in) high. Draw a horizontal line along the paper at a height of 5.5cm (2⅛in), for the decorative wall that the cat sits upon. Trace the cat onto the centre of the wall. Next, referring either to Klimt's 'Tree of Life' painting, or to the completed cake design (see page 95), sketch scrolls behind and above the cat, plus a few in front of his paws.

2. Secure your scroll design to your covered cake using glass-headed dressmakers' pins. Then carefully transfer the scroll design to the sugarpaste surface below, by running a scriber firmly over the scrolls. There is no need to scribe the cat onto the cake.

3. Dip a fine paintbrush into sugar glue and paint over the scrolls.

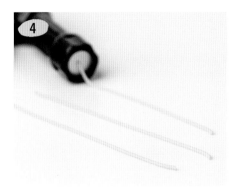

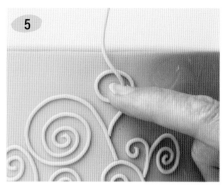

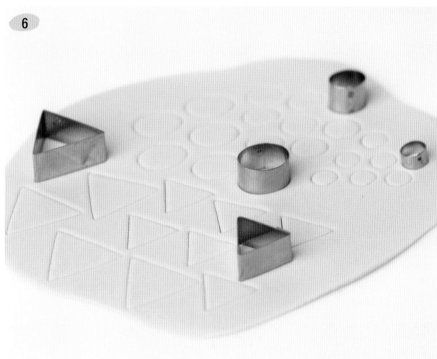

4. Soften some of the gold modelling paste by adding a little white vegetable fat and cooled boiled water. Knead until it is quite soft. Place inside the sugar shaper together with the small round disc. Push down the plunger and pump using the handle to squeeze out several lengths of paste onto your work board. If the paste doesn't come out easily, it isn't soft enough – add more white fat and water.

5. Once the lengths have firmed up a fraction and are easy to handle, position them over the painted glued scrolls, using a finger or paintbrush to aid placement. Cut to size on the cake using a craft knife. Review the shapes and adjust as necessary, using your paintbrush to give smooth curves.

6. Roll out some thin gold modelling paste and stamp out small triangles and ovals using the sugarcraft cutters.

7. Then, using sugar glue and a paintbrush, attach the cut-out geometric shapes to the cake in the area on the right of the cat, as shown on page 95.

8. To gild the cake, load a brush with white vegetable fat. Paint over all but the wall area of the cake, ensuring that the edges of the shapes and scrolls are well covered.

9. Place a selection of gold and bronze edible lustre dusts on a plate or paint palette. Load a paintbrush with one colour and start to dust over the cake as shown, changing and blending colours as you go until you have completely covered the backdrop.

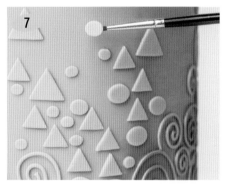

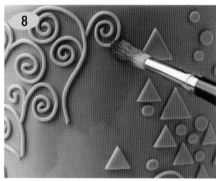

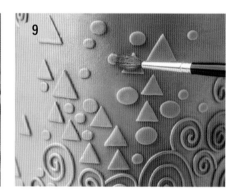

CREATING THE COLOURFUL WALL DESIGN

CONCENTRIC CIRCLE PATTERNS

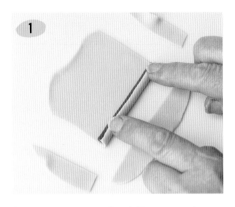

1. Choose a selection of modelling paste colours that you wish to work with. Roll the first colour into a short thin sausage. Roll the second colour thinly into a rough rectangle. Cut one edge straight with a craft knife. Paint sugar glue along this straight edge and over some of the rectangle. Place the sausage along the straight edge and roll the paste around the sausage as shown.

2. Cut away the excess paste using a craft knife. The idea is that the colours abut rather than overlap each other, to create concentric circles. Add as many layers and colours as desired. Repeat with different colourways and numbers of layers to create varied patterns of different sizes.

3. To ensure that the layers of the rolls stick together securely, they need to rest. Wrap each prepared sausage in plastic food wrap before placing in an airtight container. Set to one side while making the next elements.

MILLEFIORI PATTERNS

Millefiori is a technique originally used with glass where circular lengths of different sizes and colours are fused together and cut into sections to form patterns.

1. Choose at least four colours to make these beautiful *millefiori* patterns. Soften three of your chosen modelling paste colours, as described for the gold scrolls (see page 97). Using the large and medium discs with the sugar shaper, squeeze out paste lengths onto your work surface. You will need a central colour plus at least four of each of the other two colours. Using sugar glue, stick the lengths alternately around the central colour. It's very important that everything is well secured – you don't want your pattern to fall apart!

2. Roll the fourth and final colour thinly into a rough rectangle. Cut one edge straight with a craft knife. Paint sugar glue along this straight edge and over some of the rectangle. Lay the lengths you've just stuck together along the straight edge and roll the paste around the sausage as shown. Cut away the excess paste using a craft knife. With a smoother, roll the sausage backwards and forwards to smooth and even out the paste. Wrap in plastic food wrap and set to one side.

SPIRAL PATTERNS

Choose two or three colours of modelling paste. Roll out each thinly into a rectangle. Stick the rectangles on top of one another using sugar glue. Cut three straight edges using a craft knife, then roll the pastes to form a spiral pattern, as shown on the left.

TWO-TONE CHEQUERED PATTERN

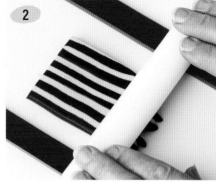

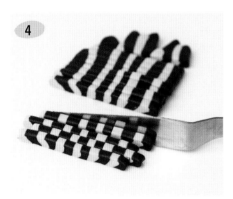

1. Use 5mm (³⁄₁₆in) spacers to roll out two colours of modelling paste. Cut each colour in half and stack them alternately to form four layers. Use a very sharp knife; a blunt one will drag the paste. Cut the resulting stack into 6mm- (¼in-) wide slices.

2. Place the slices side by side on your work surface. Using your rolling pin and the 5mm (³⁄₁₆in) spacers, roll over the stripes to elongate and even out the thickness of the stripes.

3. Take your sharp knife and cut across the resulting stripes at 5mm (³⁄₁₆in) intervals.

4. Using a palette knife, pull the first cut length a little away from the rest, across the surface of your work board. Pull the second length across but position the strip so that it starts to form a chequerboard pattern as shown. Briefly roll over the pattern in both directions with a rolling pin to secure the pieces. Cover with plastic food wrap and set to one side.

THREE-TONE CHEQUERED PATTERN

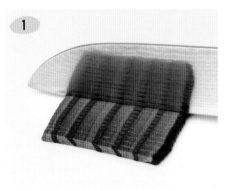

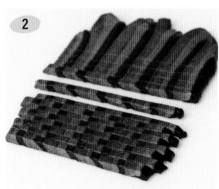

1. Repeat the same process as used for the two-tone pattern – this time, use three colours.

2. You have more pattern options with three colours, so you can experiment with the placement of your strips to see which you prefer. Alternatively, lay some one way and some another.

COLOURED CIRCLES

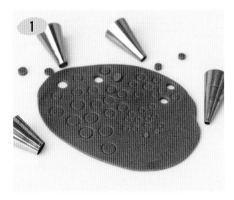

1. Roll out your remaining modelling paste, roll some thickly and some thinly. Then, with the suggested selection of piping tubes (see page 96), cut out circles of different sizes in each colour.

2. Place the gold-coloured circles onto waxed paper. Mix a little edible gold lustre dust with a little confectioners' glaze and paint over each circle to gild it.

ASSEMBLING THE WALL

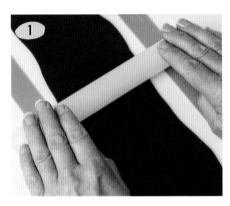

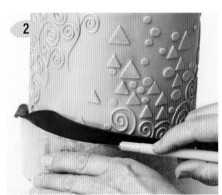

1. Roll out the black modelling paste between 1mm spacers, into a 6cm- (2⅜in-) wide strip that will be long enough to wrap around the cake.

2. Cut one long edge of the strip straight using a craft knife and a straight edge. Paint sugar glue over the wall area on the cake. Carefully pick up the black paste and wrap it around the cake, cutting the ends to size so that they abut. Note that they will be hidden by the pattern. Cut away the wall from your paper design and position it around your cake. Use a craft knife to cut away the excess paste in a nice, neat horizontal line.

3. Unwrap the prepared patterns and make slices from each, using a sharp knife.

4. Once you have all the elements ready, use a paintbrush and sugar glue to attach them to the wall to create a randomized pattern. Start with the larger shapes and fill the gaps with the smaller circles.

This isn't a flat design, so feel free to stack one shape upon another. Continue until you have completely covered the wall.

THE CAT

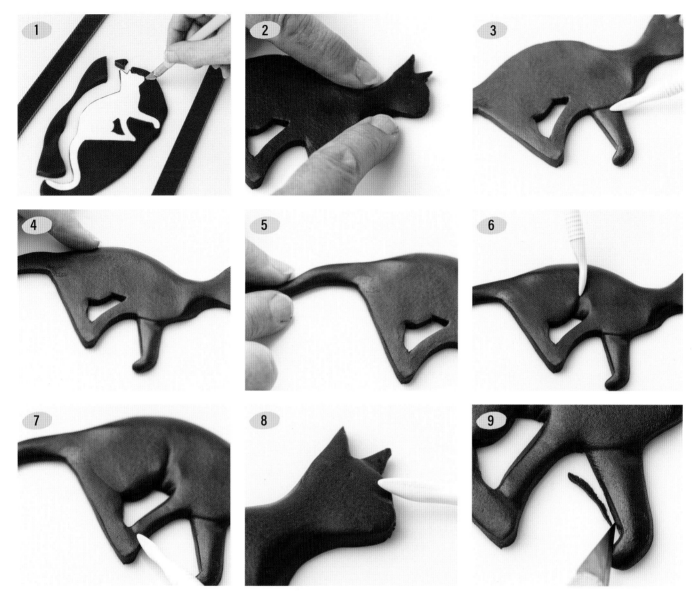

1. Roll out the remaining black modelling paste between the 5mm (³⁄₁₆in) spacers, ensuring that you roll enough to fit beneath the cat template (see page 140). Place the template on top and cut around it with a craft knife.

2. Use your fingers to smooth and shape the cat. Round off his neck by stroking two fingers over the cut edges.

3. Define the front-left leg by pressing into the paste with the flat end of a dresden tool.

4. Curve the cat's back with the heat of a finger.

5. Shape the tail in the same way.

6. Define the area between the front and back legs with the flat end of the dresden tool. Then run the tool into the paste to define the hind leg.

7. Separate the front legs from the hind legs by pressing the dresden tool into the front-right leg as shown.

8. Define the back ear and then the eye area.

9. To round off the limbs, use a craft knife to undercut sections as shown.

FINISHING TOUCHES

Attach the finished cat in position on the cake using sugar glue. Experiment with the position of his front-left paw and tail before fixing.

Place your decorated cake on the cake board and admire your handiwork!

PUFFY THE PUFFIN

Puffins are so cute and comical to watch – who could fail to
love these 'clowns of the sea'?
This design is perfect as a birthday cake for someone
who's potty about puffins – or you can add a Santa hat
to Puffy so he can become the mascot of an excellent
alternative Christmas cake (see page 111).

THE INSPIRATION

It's best to plan if you want to get up close and personal with puffins. Last summer, three
of us did just that. We got up very early one morning, at a time I'd rather not remember, and
joined the queue for the boat that would take us to Skomer Island, a bird paradise a mile off the
Pembrokeshire coast.

During puffin breeding season, such trips are incredibly popular – we were not disappointed.
We found the puffins to be incredibly entertaining, small, noisy and fast. They seemed to fly like
bullets, so I never did manage to successfully photograph one in flight!

These cheeky birds made such a big impression on me that one of them seems to have
sneaked its way into this book – thank you, Puffy!

YOU WILL NEED

MATERIALS

- Cake – 12.5cm (5in) diameter × 15cm (6in) height – baked in two halves
- Sugarpaste (fondant): 900g (2lb) white, 50g (1¾oz) dark grey, 50g (1¾oz) light grey
- Buttercream or chocolate ganache to add as a base coat before the sugarpaste (fondant)
- Royal icing – stiff consistency
- White sugar balls of different sizes
- Edible food dusts – a selection of colours including blues, green, black and white and colours for the puffin
- Modelling chocolate coloured with food dusts as follows: 90g (3⅛oz) white, 20g (¾oz) black, 5g (⅛oz) orange, 10g (⅜oz) dark orange,

10g (⅜oz) grey, 5g (⅛oz) yellow 5g (⅛oz) steel-blue, 2g (⅟₁₆in) red, 10g (⅜oz) green

- White vegetable fat
- Sugar glue (see page 17)
- Piece of dry spaghetti

EQUIPMENT

- 18cm (7in) hardboard cake board
- Puffin template × 2 (see page 141)
- Two A4 – 297 x 210mm (11¾ x 8¼in) – plastic document wallets
- 2.5cm (1in) teardrop cutter (by Lindy's Cakes)
- Smoother
- Waxed paper
- Selection of paintbrushes
- Glass-headed dressmakers' pins

- Cutting wheel
- Dresden tool
- Scissors
- Rolling pin
- Palette knife
- Ball tool
- Selection of paintbrushes – including a size 2 or 3
- White plates
- Sugar shaper (sugar extruder) and assorted discs
- Length of 5mm (³⁄₁₆in) green ribbon
- Non-toxic glue stick

PREPARING THE CAKE

Level, stack and cover your baked cakes with white sugarpaste (fondant) to create one 15cm (6in) tall cake with sharp edges, following the instructions in the Techniques section (see pages 22–24).

Place centrally on the 18cm (7in) cake board. Cut out a disc of waxed paper slightly larger than the top of your covered cake. Position it temporarily on top of your cake, weighing it down with a smoother.

Note

I used milk modelling chocolate as a base for the black, and white modelling chocolate for all the other colours.

CREATING THE SEA

1. Place some individual blue and green food dusts on a work board or white plate. Using a palette knife, add some stiff royal icing on top of each coloured dust, then blend each colour as shown.

2. Add some of your coloured royal icing to the back of your palette knife and spread it horizontally around your cake. Repeat with another colour, blending and smoothing as you go. You are not looking for a smooth finish at this stage, just a blend of colours that looks pleasing.

3. As you spread the icing, use either the board as an anchor or the smoother resting on the top of the cake. Continue until the sides of the cake are completely covered with royal icing. Note that it is not necessary to go right down to the board as this area will be covered in rocks.

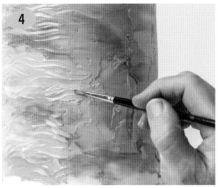

4

5

6

Tip

If you are not happy with one particular section, you can always change it by adding more icing on top of a different colour.

4. Dip a size 2 or 3 paintbrush in water. Then draw wave patterns through the wet icing.

5. Once you are happy with the effect, neaten the icing on the top edge of the cake, using your paintbrush and additional icing as required.

6. Finally, use a damp paintbrush to pick up the white sugar balls and position them at random on the wet royal icing. Allow the icing to dry.

THE ROCKS

1

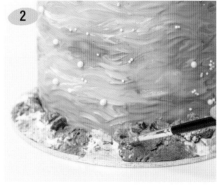

2

1. Without kneading your grey sugarpaste, tear off pieces of appropriate sizes. Attach them around the base of your cake with their torn sides uppermost to create textured rocks. Earmark an area where the puffin will stand and ensure that it is large enough for his feet!

2. Colour a small amount of royal icing orange. Using a paintbrush, dab it over small areas of the rock to represent orange lichen patches. Repeat, but this time use white royal icing.

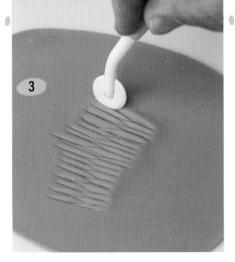

3. Warm then thinly roll out the green chocolate modelling paste. Take a cutting wheel and run it backwards and forwards over the paste to create small, thin triangles as shown. Cut along the bases of your triangles and remove the excess paste.

4. Using a dresden tool, pick up a few triangles to form a tuft of grass. Stick the grass between the crevices in the rock.

5. Mix black and green food dusts separately with a little water to make paint. Using a paintbrush, stipple it over areas of the rocks to add interest as desired.

PUFFY THE PUFFIN

Puffy is created using modelling chocolate coloured with food dusts. I know, however, that some of you have really hot hands and struggle to use modelling chocolate, in which case I suggest that you simply switch to using modelling paste – perhaps a commercial paste that doesn't dry too quickly.

THE BODY

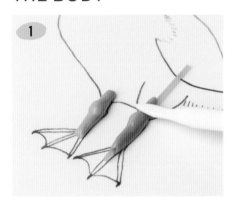

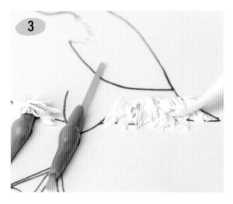

1. Place a copy of the puffin template into a plastic wallet. Warm some orange modelling chocolate, then roll two sausages for the legs. Insert a short length of dry spaghetti through one sausage. Place on the template so that the one with the spaghetti becomes Puffy's left leg. Thin either side of the knees using a dresden tool with a rocking action, until the legs fit the template.

2. To create fluffy feathers, roll out some warmed white modelling chocolate thinly. Then, taking the larger end of the cutting wheel, run it backwards and forwards along the edge of the paste as shown. Try to keep the cuts fairly close to create thin, wispy feathers. Cut a line through the modelling chocolate, about 2mm (1/16in) from the base of the feathers.

3. Using your dresden tool, pick up sections of feathers and position them around the top of Puffy's right leg and under his tail as shown. Add movement to the feathers by tweaking them with a dresden tool. No glue is needed as the warmed soft modelling chocolate sticks to itself.

> **Tip**
> Try microwaving your chocolate modelling paste for a few seconds to help warm it and make it more pliable but be careful you don't overdo it!

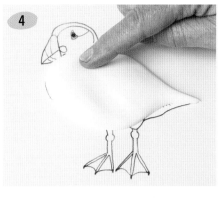

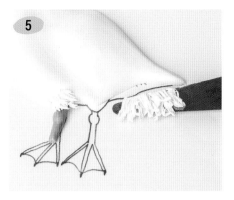

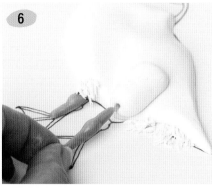

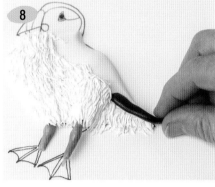

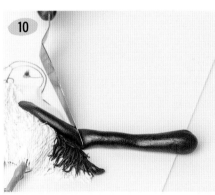

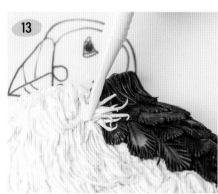

4. Place the second copy of the puffin template in a separate plastic wallet. Warm 60g (2⅛oz) of white modelling chocolate and shape it to fit the template as shown. Puffy's chest is the thickest part, and tapers down towards his legs. Shape the wing area by using the heat of your finger. Taper the tail and stroke to a point.

5. Position Puffy's right leg. Then transfer the tail feathers using a palette knife.

6. Roll approximately 5g (⅛oz) of white modelling chocolate into a thick sausage to create the top of Puffy's left leg. Then insert the leg centrally using the spaghetti. Note that the leg doesn't lie flat; it lies parallel to the template at a height of approximately 1cm (⅜in).

7. Create more fluffy feathers and add these to the chest and legs in overlapping layers as shown, changing the direction of the feathers as desired.

8. Next, add a tapered sausage of black modelling chocolate to the lower tail area.

9. Create fluffy feathers from thinly rolled black modelling chocolate, as before, and attach to the end of the tail as shown.

10. Roll a long, thick tapered sausage of black modelling chocolate. Position it on top of the rail area to form the base of the wings. Cut to size with a palette knife.

11. To make feathers, thinly roll out the black modelling chocolate and stamp out teardrops using the 2.5cm (1in) teardrop cutter. Using the small end of the cutting wheel, cut into a teardrop to create vanes. Leave the centre uncut to form the shaft or rachis as shown.

12. Arrange the prepared feathers in overlapping rows starting above the tail to form the wings, as shown.

13. Finish off at the back of the neck with black, fluffy feathers. Next, add a tuft of white ones that overlap the very top edge of the wing. Finally, complete the line of black, fluffy feathers under his neck by adding a row over the white.

THE HEAD

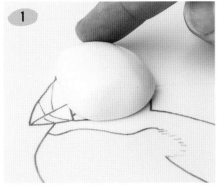

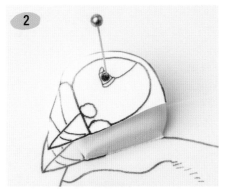

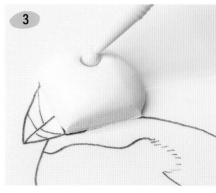

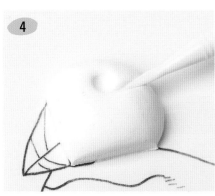

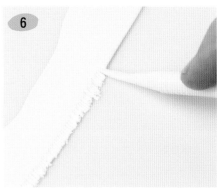

1. Warm 14g (½oz) white modelling chocolate. Roll it into a ball, then place on the head of the puffin template. Smooth the paste to shape using the heat of your fingers. The head should taper down toward the outline of the template on the top and back of the head, be rounded at the neck and have a flat area where the beak will be attached. Use a palette knife to cut away any excess paste at the neck.

2. To mark the position of the eye, cut out the head from one of the templates and, using a dressmakers' pin, mark the position of the eye.

3. Indent the eye socket using the small end of a ball tool.

4. With a dresden tool, indent the line that goes from the eye towards the back of the head.

5. Place the modelled head onto the body. Starting at the back of the neck, add black fluffy feathers in short rows to the back and top of the head as shown.

6. Warm and roll out some white modelling chocolate thinly. Cut one straight edge. Using the thin end of your dresden tool, press repeatedly into the paste to texture it. Cut away the excess paste, leaving a small border.

7. Starting at the back of the head, add textured overlapping rows as shown. Continue until all but the eye socket and beak area is covered.

8. Adjust the feathering as desired with a dresden tool.

THE BEAK

Did you know puffins shed their colourful beaks after the breeding session is over?

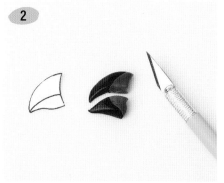

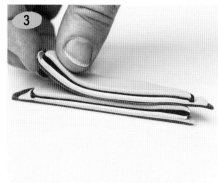

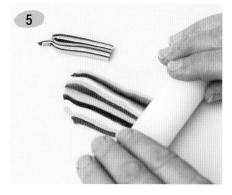

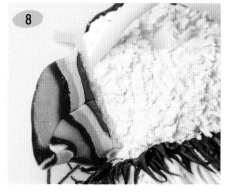

1. Cut out a copy of the beak template. Shape some orange modelling chocolate into a rough tapered beak shape. Place the template on top and adjust the shape as necessary. Cut away the excess paste using a craft knife. Repeat using the steel-blue modelling chocolate. Cut the two beaks in half horizontally to form the upper and lower beak sections.

2. Next, make diagonal cuts in each section and replace the inner orange parts with steel-blue ones as shown.

3. To make the beak stripes, roll out thin lengths of orange, grey, white, dark orange and gold paste. Stack these on top of one another. Cut in half lengthways and stack the two halves as shown.

4. Using a craft knife, cut a 2–3mm- (1/16–1/8in-) wide strip through all the layers.

5. Place this strip on your work surface and roll over it with a rolling pin to thin, widen and blend the colours.

6. Next, pick up the striped strip and place it over the orange sections of the beak as shown. Neatly cut away the excess with a craft knife.

7. Repeat the process to cover the rear of each section. Pinch the joins together along the ridge of the beak to blend and shape the beak. Next, place the two halves of the beak back together and attach to the head, angling the beak tip away from the template.

8. Texture a thin strip of pale yellow modelling chocolate and attach it around the beak where it joins the head. Add more texture using a dresden tool.

9. At either side of the base of the beak, add a small, black textured circle, then add a smaller grey one on top. Next, create the yellow gape flange at both corners of his mouth. Do this by adding a small flattened ball of paste. Add textured radial lines coming from the centre of each gape flange with a dresden tool, then texture the outside edges as shown.

THE EYE

1. Roll a small ball of red modelling chocolate just large enough to fit in the eye socket. Press the small end of your ball tool into the centre of the eye to spread the red paste.

2. Fill the cavity with a ball of grey paste, then add a black circle for the pupil. Next, add a small tapered white sausage of paste for the light spot.

3. Add the distinctive grey and black eye markings as shown.

FINISHING TOUCHES

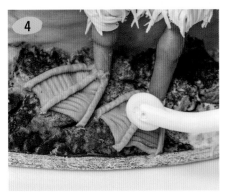

1. Pick up your completed puffin and, using royal icing, attach him in place on the cake. Bend him slightly to take up the curvature of the cake and use dressmakers' pins to hold him in place while the icing dries, as shown. When positioning also ensure that his feet, once added, will rest in a natural position.

2. Roll out some orange modelling chocolate thinly and cut out the feet using the foot templates and a cutting wheel.

3. Attach in place, then indent lines to create the webbing on the feet using a cutting wheel.

4. Add thin sausages of orange paste for toes, indenting each with a cutting wheel as shown. Then dust over the feet with a little orange dust to help highlight the texturing.

5. Finally, roll small black cones for claws and attach in place. Add a green ribbon to the edge of the cake board using a non-toxic glue stick.

A SEASONAL VARIATION

Help Puffy celebrate Christmas by creating a Santa hat for him to wear.

Shape a ball of red sugarpaste (fondant) into a cone. Bend over the top of the cone and cut away any excess from the base so that the hat looks in proportion to Puffy. Using your thumb and forefinger, pinch the edge of the base of the cone to widen it slightly. Attach it to Puffy's head and mark creases in the hat using a dresden tool.

Roll some white sugarpaste (fondant) into a pea-sized ball. Texture the ball with the pointed end of a dresden tool and attach it to the point of the hat as a pompom.

Finally, roll a sausage of white sugarpaste (fondant) and place it around the base of the hat. Texture as for the pompom.

ECHINACEA

Echinacea plants, native to the dry plains of North America, produce large beautiful daisylike flowers with sea-urchin-shaped centres. These flowers have been used in herbal medicine for thousands of years by the Native Americans. Early settlers appreciated the plant's medicinal value for treating colds and flu, and took it to Europe in the seventeenth century.

I think these stunning flowers make a perfect cake subject for, say, a garden enthusiast, plant lover, flower arranger, herbalist, alternative therapist or anyone who admires natural beauty.

The life-like petals, leaves and buds are easily created using homemade or commercially available veiners and moulds so they are not as tricky to make as you might think.

THE INSPIRATION

While creating the designs that you'll find on these pages, I asked my Facebook followers what they would most like to see in this book. One of the most popular suggestions was a floral birthday cake. But which flower should I choose? I wanted to use a less obvious flower than a rose, a sweet pea, a dahlia – something striking yet beautiful, colourful yet delicate. I looked to see what was growing right outside my studio: lots of gorgeous, colourful flowers including echinaceas. I've tried growing echinacea from seed on and off for years. This year, however, was the first time I managed to beat the damp and the slugs.
I am very pleased with my achievement, so much so that these flowers have become the subject of this design. Incidentally, they also inspired a wet-felted picture I was making at the same time – the power of inspiration!
I hope these flowers appeal to you too.

1. Close-up of an echinacea centre;
2. An echinacea bud;
3. Echinacea in full bloom.

YOU WILL NEED

MATERIALS

- Cake – 15cm (6in) diameter × 19cm (7.5in) height
- 1kg (2¼lb) white sugarpaste (fondant)
- Buttercream or chocolate ganache to add as a base coat before the sugarpaste (fondant)
- Airbrush colours: orange, yellow, pink, green, teal
- Flower paste green, yellow, burgundy, pink
- Edible food dusts: a selection of greens, purple, red, pink
- White vegetable fat
- Sugar glue (see page 17)
- Green royal icing – small amount
- Paste colours – orange and burgundy

EQUIPMENT AND TOOLS

- 23cm (9in) cake board
- Airbrush
- Echinacea flower and leaf images
- Fresh echinacea flower petals and leaves to make veiners (or commercially available veiners)
- Two-part silicone mould-making kit (if you are making your own veiners)
- Grooved flower-making board
- Self-healing cutting mat
- Craft knife
- Wire cutters
- Flat-nose jewellery pliers
- Tea-light
- Cutters:
  - 2.5cm (1in) teardrop cutter (by Lindy's Cakes)
  - 5cm (2in) pointed oval cutter (by Lindy's Cakes)
- Floristry wires: 33-gauge green, 24-gauge green, 18-gauge green, 26-gauge white
- Green floristry tape
- Steam source: steamer or pan of simmering water
- Smoother
- Foam pad
- Waffle foam
- Glass-headed dressmakers' pins
- Cutting wheel
- Dresden tool
- Scissors
- Rolling pin
- Ball tool
- Selection of paintbrushes
- White plate or paint palette
- Sugar shaper (sugar extruder) and assorted discs
- Kitchen paper
- Narrow ribbon to cover the edge of the board
- Non-toxic glue stick

MAKING MOULDS

USING PETAL AND LEAF VEINERS AND MAKING THE BUD CENTRE

1. Select suitable fresh leaves and petals from an echinacea plant or stem. Following the instructions that come with your mould-making kit, mix up and blend enough silicone to create the bases of your leaves and petals. Divide up the mixture and roll out into suitable shapes. Take a leaf and carefully press it into the silicone mix, taking care to exclude all the air. Repeat for the additional leaves, then the petals. Allow the silicone to dry with the leaves and petals in place.

2. Once dry, carefully spread a thin layer of white vegetable fat over the exposed area of the silicone around each leaf and petal. Mix up more of the two-part silicone mix and carefully position some on top of each leaf and petal. Try to ensure that you don't trap any air in the process. Leave to dry. Once dry, lift off the top sections of each veiner and remove the leaf or petal. Your veiners are now ready to use.

3. To create a bud mould, simple mix up a small amount of silicone and press it onto the surface of a fresh bud. Allow to dry before carefully peeling away the mould.

ECHINACEA BUDS

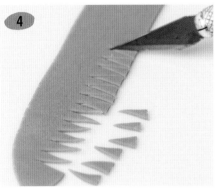

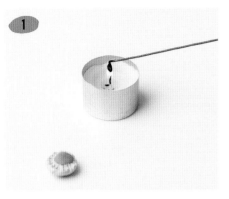

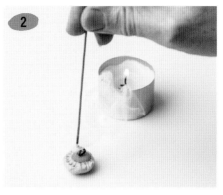

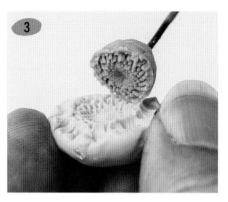

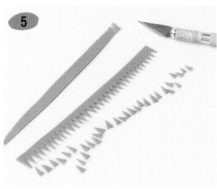

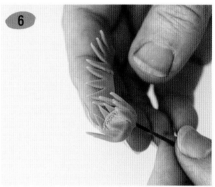

1. Using flat-nosed jewellery pliers, bend the tip of a 15cm- (6in-) long 18-gauge wire over to make an 'O' shape. Clamp the 'O' in the mouth of the pliers and bend it through 90 degrees. Firmly press a small ball of green flower paste into your prepared bud mould; alternatively, use a 1.2cm- (½in-) wide daisy centre mould. Heat the shaped tip of your wire in the flame of a tea-light until it is red hot.

2. Quickly insert the wire into the back of the bud. The heat will melt the sugar and, once cooled, will ensure a firm connection between the wire and bud.

3. Pick up the bud and gently peel away the textured bud from the mould.

4. Roll some green flower paste into a thin, narrow strip. Then using your craft knife cut away small triangles as shown.

5. Cut away the excess paste at the back of the triangles to leave a border approximately 3–5mm (⅛–³⁄₁₆in) wide.

6. Next, wrap the strip around the edge of the bud, using sugar glue to stick, so that the points of the triangles sit above the centre. Repeat until you have three layers of small triangles wrapped around the centre.

7. Thinly roll out another strip of green flower paste. Cut the edges straight. Then use the 2.5cm (1in) narrow teardrop cutter to cut long thin triangles as shown. Place these triangles on a foam pad and gently run the small end of a ball tool from the tip to the base of each to curve and shape.

8. Using sugar glue, attach these shaped triangles around the outside of the bud, so that they curve away from the centre. Build up the layers in rows, positioning the triangles in the spaces left by the previous row. Build up three layers, using a dresden tool to aid placement.

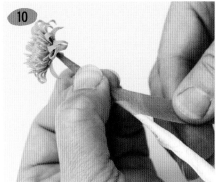

9. Wrap a small piece of white kitchen paper carefully around the wire below the bud.

10. Stretch the end of the tape to release the glue, then wrap it tightly around the top of the wire immediately under the bud. Once it is holding firmly, continue stretching and winding the tape around the padded wire. Add more layers directly under the bud to add bulk, as this area of the stem is wider than the rest. Finally, add another layer of tape over the first to thicken up the stem further. Repeat the above to make the second bud, this time using the full length of the wire.

MAKING LEAVES

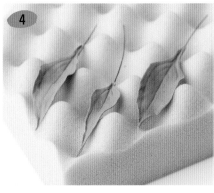

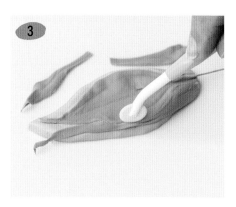

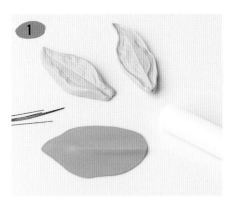

1. Cut three lengths of 24-gauge wire into four shorter lengths each. Roll out some green flower paste thickly, enough for one leaf. Then, using a small rolling pin, thin either side of the centre to create a thicker central ridge.

2. Dip one of the cut wires into glue, then insert into this central ridge. Then place into one side of one of your leaf veiners, positioning the wire so it corresponds with the vein in the leaf. Add the second side of the veiner on top, carefully lining it up with the first. Press down firmly to imprint the veins on both side of your sugar leaf. Carefully release the top veiner by peeling it away.

3. With a cutting wheel, cut away the excess paste from around the edges of the leaf.

4. Place the leaf on a foam pad. Then run the large end of a ball tool, half on the leaf and half on the pad, gently around the edges to soften the cut. Place on waffle foam to dry. Repeat to make approximately nine leaves.

5. Once the leaves have firmed up, it's time to colour them using food dust colours. Place your chosen greens and a purple on a white plate or paint palette. Load up your brush and dust areas of your leaves with suitable colours. Dust both the back and front of each leaf, using my examples or fresh leaves to guide you. To bring the leaves to life, dust the edges with the purple dust.

6. Steam each leaf to help set the dusts, using either a pan of simmering water (a) or a steamer (b).

ECHINACEA CENTRES: THE FLOWER CONES

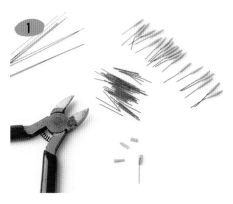

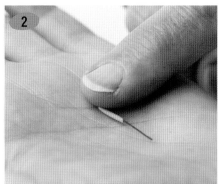

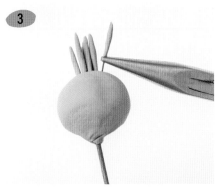

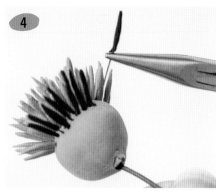

1. Cut the 33-gauge wire into 2cm (¾in) lengths. Roll some of the yellow flower paste into a thin sausage and cut into short 3–5mm (⅛–³⁄₁₆in) lengths. Dip one end of a wire into glue and place on top of one of the small lengths as shown.

2. Place in the palm of your hand and roll it backwards and forwards to spread the paste over and along the wire. Repeat. For the two flowers, you will need approximately 150 yellow and 50 or so burgundy.

3. Roll a 1.5cm (⁹⁄₁₆in) ball of flower paste and insert a hot wire, following the same method as for the bud (see page 115). Once the paste is firmly fixed to the wire, use flat-nosed pliers to position the covered wires. Start with the yellow ones, grouping them so that they point to the centre as can be seen on the finished flower, below.

4. Continue adding the yellow wires, gradually changing their direction so that they start to point slightly away from the centre. Once you've added enough, probably about 100, change to the burgundy colour and insert a ring of these around the yellow ones.

Note

At step 4, using a sugar shaper may speed up the process, but this does mean that, once dry, these parts of the flower will not be moveable.

5. Warm and soften some of the burgundy paste by adding a little white fat and water. Once it is soft, place it into a sugar shaper fitted with the large mesh disc. Squeeze out lengths and attach them around the others as shown.

6. Repeat to make the flower centre that rests against the cake. Note that you need make only half a cone.

7. Dilute some of the burgundy and orange paste colours separately, with a little water. Take a paintbrush and paint the top half of each composite flower with the orange as shown.

8. Lightly touch the top of each with burgundy.

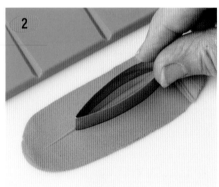

ECHINACEA PETALS

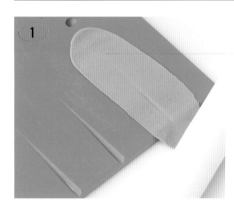

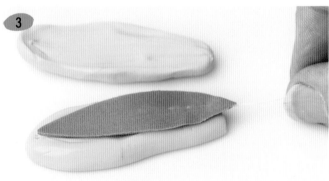

1. Roll out some pink flower paste thinly over a groove on the flower-making board as shown.

2. Remove the paste and flip it over to reveal the central ridge in the paste. Take the 5cm (2in) pointed oval cutter and cut out an oval so that the ridge runs down the centre, as shown.

3. Cut the white wires into 10cm (4in) lengths. Dip one of the cut wires into glue then insert into this central ridge. Place the wired oval on one side of a petal veiner.

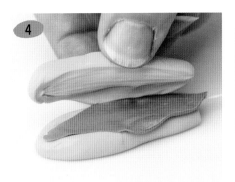

Tip

You may find it easier to line up the veiner if you mark both sides with a pencil line, for example.

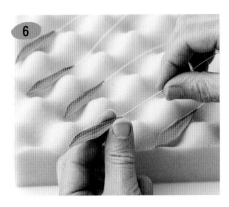

4. Line up the second half of the petal veiner and press down firmly. Remove the top veiner.

5. With a cutting wheel, cut away the excess paste from around the edges of the petal.

6. Place the petal on a foam pad, then gently run the large end of a ball tool, half on the petal and half on the pad, around the edges to soften the cut. Pinch the base of the petal together with your fingers before placing on waffle foam to dry. Repeat to make approximately twenty-five petals.

7. Once the petals have firmed up, it's time to colour. Place your red, pink and purple dusts onto a white plate or paint palette. Load up your brush with the red colour and dust about half of the petal as shown. Over-dust with the pink, taking the colour further up towards the tip, then add purple to the base. Finally, add a light dusting of pale green to the back of each petal.

8. Steam the petals to help set the dusts, using either a pan of simmering water or a steamer, as for the leaves.

ASSEMBLING THE FLOWERS

1. Establish how you'd like the petals to sit against the cone, then bend each wire so it will abut the central stem neatly. Start taping the petals in place, adding one at a time and gradually building up until you have approximately nine for the half flower and fourteen for the full flower. Thicken up the stem using kitchen paper as for the bud and tape as before.

2. Finally, add the three layers of green teardrops, as you did for the bud, positioning the first row so that they can be seen through the petals where possible. Blend the paste from the final row into the stem.

FINISHING OFF THE STEMS

You should now have two flower stems and two bud stems. Use floristry tape to add leaves, placing them at 180 degrees to each other alternately down each stem (see right). Refer to the finished cake on page 113 or a live plant for guidance.

Once completed, dust over sections of the stem with burgundy dust, then, using a very fine paintbrush, paint short vertical lines down sections of the stems.

PREPARING AND AIRBRUSHING THE CAKE

Level, stack and cover your baked cakes with white sugarpaste (fondant) to create one 19cm (7.5in) tall cake with sharp edges, following the instructions in the Techniques section (see pages 22–24).

Place your covered cake centrally on the 23cm (9in) cake board. Roll out the remaining white sugarpaste (fondant) into a long strip, long enough to fit around your cake board. Cut one edge straight. With the cut edge abutting your decorated cake, position the paste strip on the cake board. Cut to fit and blend the join with the heat of your hand. Cut away the excess from the edge of the board using a palette knife.

1. Either photograph an echinacea stem or download an online image. Resize the leaves to 7–9cm (2¾–3½in) and the flower to approximately 6cm (2⅜in) wide. Cut around each outline using a craft knife and a self-healing mat.

2. Pin your cut-out flowers and leaves to the sides of your cake using glass-headed dressmakers' pins. Position them as shown around the top third of the cake.

3. Fill your airbrush inkwell with yellow airbrush colour (see page 27) and apply the colour using a circular movement of your hand to the top half of your cake as shown. You are not trying to achieve an all-over uniform effect – the paint should be thicker in some places than others.

4. Using the pins, remove the paper flowers and leaves and reposition them further down the cake. Then gently airbrush some orange over the leaves and flowers as shown, again allowing the paint to be thicker in areas.

Tip

If you are new to airbrushing, remember to experiment on paper first until you are confident that you can achieve the effect you want.

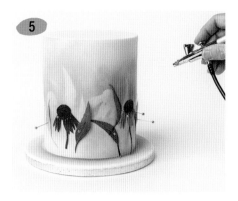

5

6

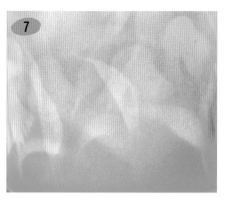

7

5. Reposition the flowers and leaves once again and this time overspray with pink using gentle circular movements.

6. Reposition the flower and leaf masks so that they abut your covered board. Add green colour to your airbrush and spray the lower sections of the cake, using a sheet of paper to mask the top of the cake.

7. Repeat step 6 using the teal colour. Once you are happy with the result, remove all the pins and paper leaves from your cake and allow your airbrushing to dry.

FINISHING TOUCHES

Decide which is the front of your cake and how you'd like to display your flowers. Bend the stems as required – the stems on the flowers in my garden seem to have a natural curve, while others I've seen are very straight.

Once you are ready, insert the tallest flower stem into the board using green royal icing to secure. Then secure where the stem touches the cake, using glass-headed dressmakers' pins to hold in place while the royal icing dries.

Repeat for the remaining stems until your display is complete.

TOADSTOOLS

Toadstools are autumn's bounty – they seem to appear
overnight, as if by magic, and then are gone in the blink
of an eye! A similar concept to birthdays, which appear to
spring upon us all of a sudden, but are quickly over.

THE INSPIRATION

Like many children, I grew up with the stories of Alice in Wonderland and other enchanting
tales of life on the forest floor. I never saw a fairy or a pixie sitting on a toadstool, but I still
can't help but think I might every time I happen to see a toadstool or two!
The fly agaric, or fairytale fungus, that I've used as the focal point of this cake was
inspired by a chance encounter last autumn. A few of these species were growing on
a woody bank, under a birch tree, close to my home. Their red caps with their distinctive
white spots simply 'jumped out' at me! I had to recreate them.
I decided to keep the colour palette minimal for the cake, so as not to detract from the
bright red caps. I achieved this by using a fluid writer and black liquid food colour to add
the details – a technique that I feel gives just the right effect. Do adapt and personalize my
design as much as you like; add a fairy, pixie, butterfly or spider, as you wish!

1. *Fly agaric* (Amanina muscaria) *or fairytale fungus;*

2. *Wood blewit* (Clitocybe nuda): *an edible mushroom
   that sometimes grows in circles called 'fairy rings';*

3. *Shaggy ink cap* (Coprinus comatus).

YOU WILL NEED

MATERIALS

- Cake – 15cm (6in) diameter × 12.5cm (5in)
- Sugarpaste (fondant) 800g (1¾lb) white, 150g (5¼oz) red
- 50g (1¾oz) white modelling paste
- Buttercream or chocolate ganache to add as a base coat before the sugarpaste (fondant)
- Black water-based airbrush or liquid colour
- Sugar glue (see page 17)

EQUIPMENT

- 20cm (8in) cake board
- Template (see page 142)
- A4 – 297 x 210mm (11¾ x 8¼in) – plastic document wallet
- Smoother
- Palette knife
- Foam pad
- 7.5cm (3in) circle cutter (optional)
- Craft knife
- Cutting wheel
- Dresden tool
- Flat-headed silicone modelling tool (optional)
- Scissors
- Rolling pin
- Ball tool
- Selection of paintbrushes
- Fluid writer (see below)
- Narrow ribbon to cover the edge of the board
- Non-toxic glue stick

PREPARING THE CAKE

Level, stack and cover your baked cakes with white sugarpaste to create one 12.5cm (5in) tall cake with sharp edges, following the instructions in the Techniques section (see pages 22–24).

Place your covered cake centrally on the 20cm (8in) cake board. Roll out the remaining white sugarpaste into a long strip, long enough to fit around your cake board. Cut one edge straight. With the cut edge abutting your decorated cake, position the paste strip on the cake board. Cut to fit and blend the join with the heat of your hand. Cut away the excess from the edge of the board using a palette knife.

Tip

To use a fluid writer successfully, you will need to ensure that your cake surface is beautifully smooth and free from any cracking. It also needs to be free from both icing sugar and white vegetable fat. If any icing sugar is present, the ink will spread to places you don't want, and if any white vegetable fat is on the surface, the ink will pool rather than stay in lines. Also, be aware that our hands are naturally greasy so don't overuse them to polish your cake either! Try rolling out your paste on a non-stick surface and using a brand of sugarpaste (fondant) that will give you a smooth finish, one with a little gum added – it is probably worth paying a little extra for this.

CREATING THE TOADSTOOLS

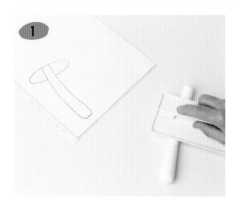

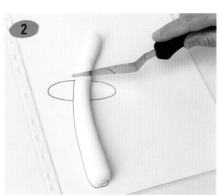

1. Copy the template twice and place one copy in a plastic document wallet. Roll some white sugarpaste into a thick sausage to fit the stem template. You might find it easier to roll the sausage with the help of a smoother. I generally find that using a smoother avoids fingermarks and gives a smooth, tapered shape. Press lightly and roll the smoother backwards and forwards along the sausage.

2. Place the stem on the template and cut off the excess from the top. You are aiming to keep the base of the stem rounded.

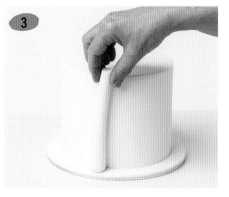

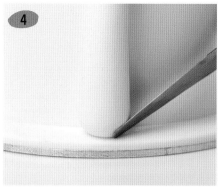

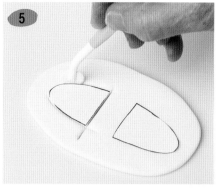

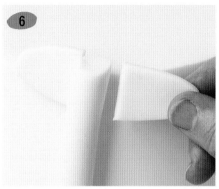

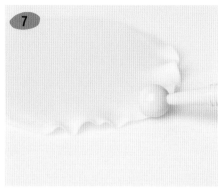

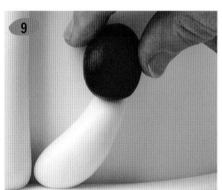

3. Stick in position on the cake using sugar glue, making sure that there is a slight curve to the stem. Note that the top of the stem is higher than the cake.

4. If the base of your stem is a little flat, use a palette knife to give it a more rounded appearance.

5. Thickly roll out some white modelling paste. Cut out the gills from the second copy of the template and place onto the paste. Cut around each with a cutting wheel.

6. Attach a gill on either side of the stem at the top of the cake using sugar glue to secure.

7. Roll out some white modelling paste thinly and cut out a 7.5cm (3in) circle. Place the circle on a foam pad and frill about half of the edge. Do this by placing a ball tool half on the paste and half on the pad and then running the tool around the edge, while gently pressing down.

8. Cut the circle in half. Pick up the frilled half from the centre of the circle and drape it over the top of the stem. Encourage folds to form in the paste and adjust until the paste resembles the skirt/ring/annulus of the toadstool, as shown.

9. Roll a white sugarpaste tapered stem for the smaller toadstool, keeping the base rounded as before. Attach in place on the side of the cake using sugar glue. Take 12g (⅜oz) of red sugarpaste, warm it, roll it into a ball, elongate this ball slightly and attach it to the top of the short stem.

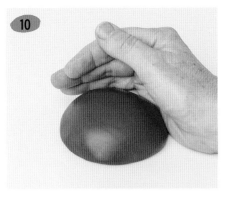

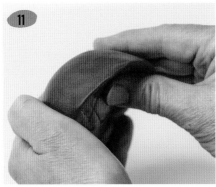

10. To make the cap of the larger toadstool, take the remaining red sugarpaste. Roll it into a smooth ball. Place the ball on your work surface, flatten slightly, then using your hand smooth the edges of the ball down to your work board to create the distinctive cap shape, as shown.

11. Release the cap from your work surface using a palette knife. Holding the cap in your hands, pinch the edge to thin and stretch the paste. Continue until half of the cap's edge has been stretched and thinned.

12. Carefully place the cap on top of its stalk, so that the unthinned section rests on the cake and the thinned section protrudes away from the cake. Ensure that the gills are neatly covered.

13. Smooth and adjust the shape of the cap as required. Allow the cap to firm up.

14. To add the spots, roll balls of white paste, some small and some large. Attach the larger ones to the top of the toadstool and the smaller ones in rings to the lower edge of the cap. Flatten each ball onto the cap as you attach it with a finger, then take a flat-headed silicone modelling tool and adjust the shape as required. The small spots should be elongated (a) and the edges of the larger spots brought down to the cap's surface (b). A soft silicone modelling tool isn't essential here; it simply makes adjusting the shapes easier.

15. Add spots to the smaller toadstool – refer to the finished cake (see page 123) for guidance.

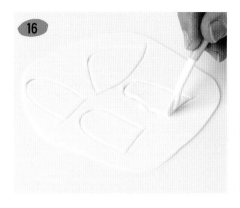

16. To create the toadstools that fill the background of the cake, roll out some white modelling paste. Cut out toadstool cap shapes freehand using a cutting wheel. Refer to the finished cake for sizes and shapes and look online for more inspiration.

17. Using sugar glue, attach each of your cut-out caps to the sides of the cake, as shown.

USING A FLUID WRITER

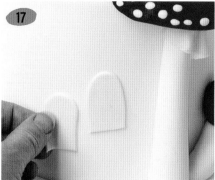

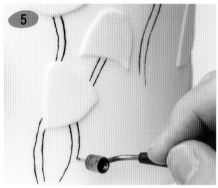

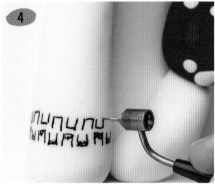

> **Note**
>
> As long as the nib of the fluid writer is at 90 degrees to the cake, you can hold the handle at any angle.

1. Before you start, take the cap off the fluid writer and place it under a running tap to force water through the nib. Next, load the fluid writer with the black water-based liquid food/airbrush colour by using a paintbrush to gradually fill the well. Try to avoid creating air bubbles in the well if possible. Place the writer on a piece of kitchen paper (paper towel) to help draw the ink through the nib. Once the ink is following freely, you are ready to start.

2. The secrets of success with a fluid writer are to make sure you use a light touch, that the surface you are writing on is dry and that you hold the fluid writer at 90 degrees to that surface. Practise on paper first: if it scratches, then you are pressing too hard – the ink should flow easily, as from an old-fashioned fountain pen. Begin by adding dots to the skirt of the toadstool.

3. Add black lines to form the gills.

4. At the base of the stem, draw open boxes as shown. Add a few short vertical lines to the base of each to add depth.

5. Draw stems for some of the white toadstool caps.

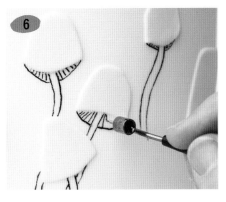

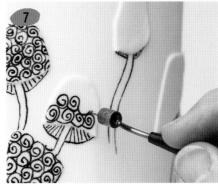

6. Add gills to the base of each cap.

7. Add patterns to decorate the caps – in my example, I've used lines of scrolls. If you are unsure of what to draw or what will work, simply try out your ideas on paper first. Design simple elements or be more adventurous. Think about what you would be drawing if you were absent-mindedly doodling – would those doodles work here?

8. Remember that you can colour sections or backgrounds and leave some areas blank.

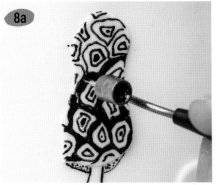

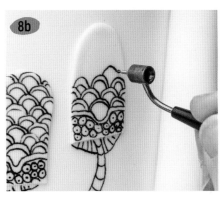

9. These toadstools can be as simple or as intricate as you wish: have some fun with them – you are not trying to draw realistic toadstools. If you go wrong, simply make the error part of the pattern. It's easy to hide your mistakes when doodling!

10. Next, start to fill in the spaces between the toadstools with smaller clusters of fungi. If you are following my design, draw the stems, add black gills, then draw a circle to create the cap. Add dots and dashes as desired.

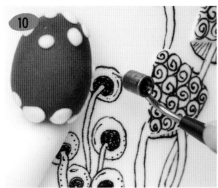

11. You could also use a chequerboard pattern to decorate some of the caps.

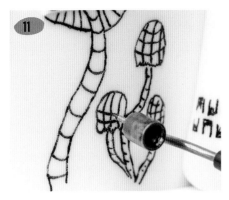

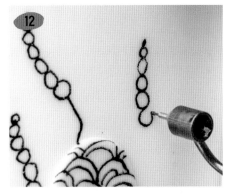

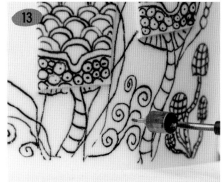

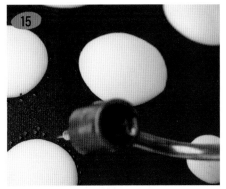

Tip

If your fluid writer gets clogged, simply insert the wire that comes with the writer into the well from above. Use some kitchen paper to clean the wire before removing it from the well again.

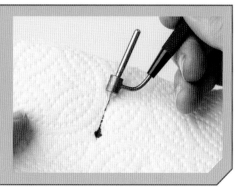

12. For the background vegetation, draw stacks of small, tapering open circles, then add waving, intertwining stems.

13. To fill the gaps between the toadstools, add single or multiple scrolls. There is no need to fill all the space, however.

14. Add any other details that you wish to. I've added a snail, but other little creatures would work just as well.

15. Finish off the red toadstools by adding black dots around each white spot on the caps.

FINISHING TOUCHES

1. Roll small white balls of sugarpaste of differing sizes and scatter them around the base of the cake. Secure with sugar glue.

2. Using your fluid writer, add dots to one side of the stones to create shadows.

Attach a suitable ribbon to the edge of your board using a non-toxic glue stick.

WINTER WONDERLAND

Who can resist a snowy winter scene, where the snow sparkles like a million tiny suns? I find snow rather thrilling and exciting, partly because, where I live, it falls only occasionally. Call me romantic, but I think of snowflakes as little kisses fluttering down from the heavens. Even now, I still love trying to catch them.

This winter wonderland design would make a perfect winter wedding or anniversary cake. It would of course also be appropriate for Christmas.

THE INSPIRATION

The design for this cake came about in a rather unusual way. It originally started life as an autumnal tree cake design, inspired by the work of a local artist. However, various transitional stages over the course of a couple of weeks turned it from an autumn abstract design that I couldn't quite get to work to a realistic winter scene. The airbrushed background was the deciding factor: it looks just like the moonrises I occasionally see here where I live (1). The tree silhouette for this design (2) comes from a nearby oak wood that I can see from my office window. In this same wood, I sometimes have the privilege of spying a small herd of deer (3). It seemed very appropriate, therefore, to add a couple of these elegant creatures to finish off the design. I'm really pleased with the design and I hope it is one that you, too, would like to create this winter.

YOU WILL NEED

MATERIALS

- Cake – 18cm (7in) diameter × 18cm (7in) height
- 1.2kg (2⅝lb) white sugarpaste (fondant)
- Buttercream or chocolate ganache to add as a base coat before the sugarpaste (fondant)
- Modelling paste: white
- White vegetable fat
- Sugar glue (see page 17)
- Airbrush colours: lilac, blue, teal and silver
- White edible dust
- Cocoa butter

- 50g (1¾oz) pastillage
- Royal icing (optional)

EQUIPMENT AND TOOLS

- 25cm (10in) cake board
- Photograph of a tree
- Deer templates (see page 143)
- Two A4 – 297 x 210mm (11¾ x 8¼in) – plastic document wallets
- 6.5cm (2½in) paper circle for the moon
- Waxed paper/tracing paper
- Pencil and eraser
- Glass-headed dressmakers' pins
- Veining tool

- Two smoothers
- Scriber
- Craft knife
- Self-healing cutting mat
- 1mm- (⅟₁₆in-) spacers
- Selection of paintbrushes
- Scissors
- Rolling pin
- Palette knife
- Foam pad
- Small nail file
- Ribbon
- Non-toxic glue stick

CREATING THE DEER

The deer should be created in advance so that the pastillage can dry thoroughly.

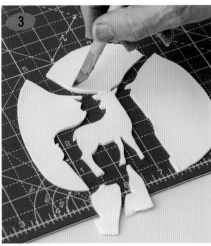
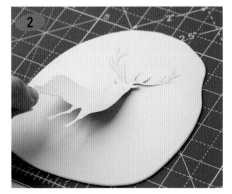

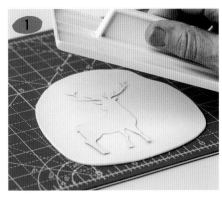

1. Create paper templates for the deer. Smear a little white vegetable fat onto your cutting mat. Roll out some pastillage and place onto your greased cutting mat. Position the stag template on top of the pastillage and press down with a smoother to emboss the stag into the pastillage.

2. Remove the template.

3. Carefully cut around the embossed shape with a craft knife, taking great care when cutting out the delicate antlers. Use a palette knife to lift the deer and carefully place it on a foam pad to dry thoroughly. Repeat steps 1 to 3 for the doe.

4. Once dry, you can smooth any uneven edges with a small nail file, but be careful – pastillage, although strong, is brittle. To strengthen the delicate antlers of your stag, add a little royal icing to them with a paintbrush.

MAKING THE TREE TEMPLATE

To create your tree template, start by photographing an interesting tree. I suggest going into a wood or park where you can find established mature trees. Choose a tree whose trunk and branches create interesting shapes. Walk around your chosen tree, photographing it from the angles that most appeal to you. I have chosen an oak tree but I am sure you'll be able to find equally interesting specimens.

Print out your tree photograph and place it on a cutting mat. With a craft knife, cut carefully around all the major branches (as shown) to create a template.

Tip

If time is short, an alternative to taking your own photograph is to source a suitable image online. Using an image manipulation program, resize your tree to fit your cake. Your branches should wrap around the sides of the cake and the upper branches should reach up beyond the top edge.

COVERING THE CAKE AND ADDING THE TREE

Level, stack and cover your baked cakes with white sugarpaste (fondant) to create one 18cm (7in) tall cake with sharp edges, following the instructions in the Techniques section (see pages 22–24).

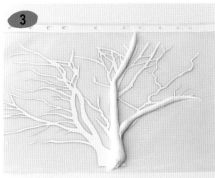

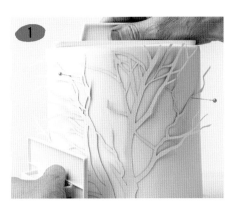

1. Immediately pin the cut-out tree template onto the cake using dressmakers' pins. Place a disc of waxed paper and smoother on top of the cake; then, using both hands as shown, press the branches of the template into the soft paste to emboss the tree outline onto the cake.

2. Use a veining tool to emboss the lines of the main trunk as shown.

3. Unpin the tree template and place inside a plastic document wallet. Roll out lengths of white sugarpaste to create the trunk and main branches of the tree. Place the branches on the template and adjust their size and shape before attaching in place on the cake.

4. Once you are happy that you've added enough branches, press the veining tool into the trunk and branches to create textured bark.

AIRBRUSHING THE CAKE AND ADDING WHITE BRANCHES

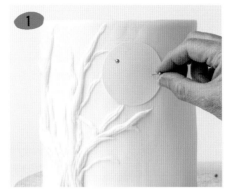

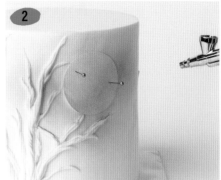

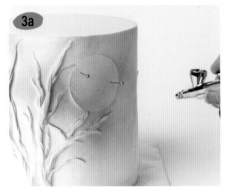

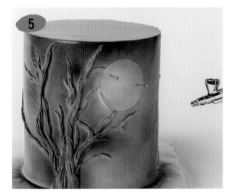

1. Pin the 6.5cm (2½in) paper circle to the cake where the upper branches of the tree will be. This circle will help create the moon.

2. Place a few drops of violet airbrush colour into the well of your airbrush before gently misting over and around the paper circle. Keep the airbrush at a reasonable distance from the cake so that you achieve a misted effect.

3. Add blue airbrush colour and gently spray around the violet, gradually adding more and more colour.

4. Add some teal and carefully mist over lower sections of the cake, avoiding the violet moon area.

5. Add some more violet to your airbrush and overspray areas on the branches and trunk. You will find that the violet and blue mix to create a gorgeous dark blue.

6. Remove the paper circle to reveal the moon.

7. Overspray lightly with blue at the top of the moon and violet on the bottom to create a misty moon feel.

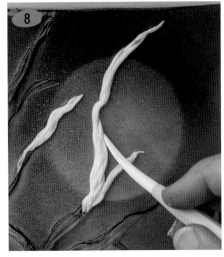

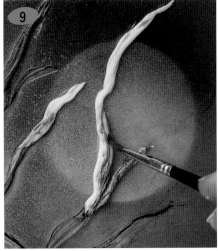

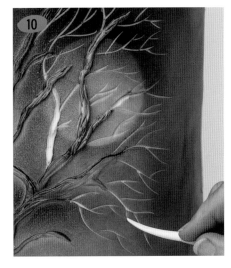

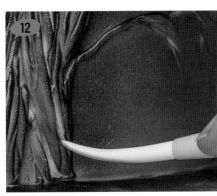

8. Using sugarpaste, add a few branches over the moon so that it appears to be behind the tree. Texture as before.

9. Paint over the branches using the violet and blue airbrush colours.

10. Next, using the embossed branch outlines for guidance, create white branches with the veining tool. For thinner branches, simply press and drag the tool through the soft icing.

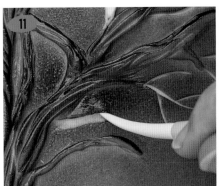

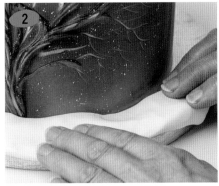

11. For the wider white branches, hold the tool at an angle before moving it across the surface of the icing. Continue until you are happy with your overall tree shape.

12. Add more detail to the trunk by again pressing the veining tool into and through the soft paste to create interest and texture, and to reveal some of the white sugarpaste beneath.

ADDING SNOW AND DEER

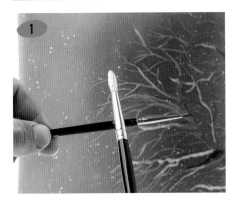

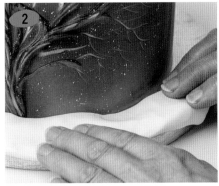

1. Melt a little cocoa butter and mix in some white dust. Generously load a paintbrush, then firmly tap this paintbrush handle onto another – the idea is to splatter small dots of white snow over the cake.

2. Use the remaining white sugarpaste to create snowdrifts on the cake board. Stroking the paste into shape with the heat of your fingers. Blend the joins so that they don't show and trim to fit, using a palette knife.

3. While the snowdrifts are still soft, insert the deer in position, as shown. Secure in place with a little royal icing.

FINISHING TOUCHES

Add a ribbon to your cake board. Secure it in place with a non-toxic glue stick.

TEMPLATES

All templates are produced full size.

DANCING IN THE RAIN

See pages 46–53.

DANDELION CLOCK

Parachute template.
See pages 54–63.

BRENDA THE BRANDHILL SHEEP

See pages 64–75.

'SARAH'S MIRACLE':
BABY SHOWER

See pages 76–85.

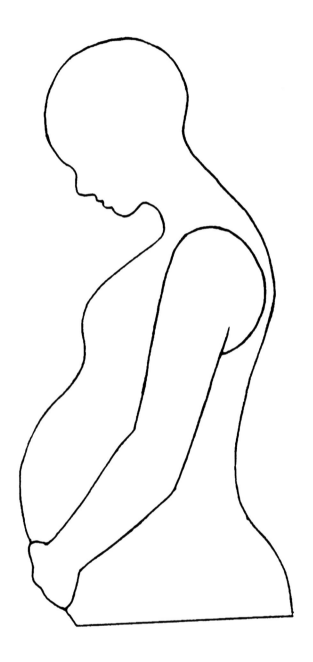

50 AND FABULOUS

See pages 86–93.

KLIMT'S CAT

See pages 94–101.

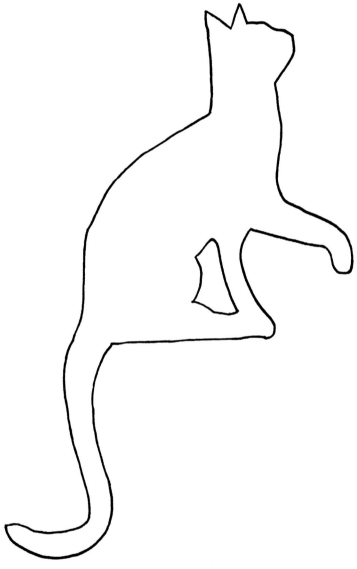

PUFFY THE PUFFIN

See pages 102–111.

TOADSTOOLS

See pages 122–129. Make two copies. Cut out the gills on the second copy for use at step 5 on page 125.

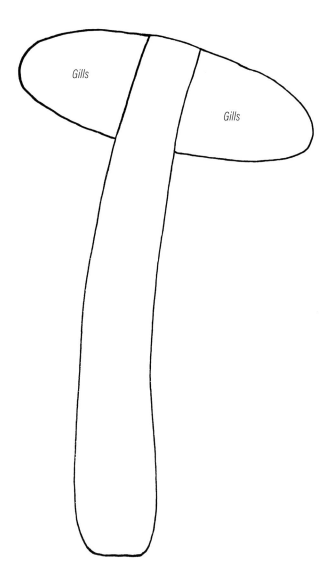

Gills

Gills

WINTER WONDERLAND

See pages 130–135.

INDEX